CHANGING
WITH
FAMILIES

by
Richard Bandler
John Grinder
and
Virginia Satir

A Book

About

Further Education For

Being Human

Science and Behavior Books, Inc.
Palo Alto, California 94306

Library of Congress Card Number 76-15450
ISBN 8314-0051-X

Typography by Penguin ≈ Santa Clara, California

To

Bob Spitzer,

who has made possible

so much of the actualization

of our creativity.

Table of Contents

About This Book and Us vii

Preface 1

PART I

    Introduction 9

    Patterns of Effective Family Therapy, Level I . . . 12

    Patterns of Effective Family Therapy, Level II . . . 54

    Summary 86

PART II

    Introduction 95

    Calibrated Communication Cycle 101

    Feedback Communication Cycle 112

    Gathering Information 117

    Transforming the System 137

    Consolidating Changes 166

    Summary 173

Epilogue 179

Further Reading 181

Bibliography 185

About This Book and Us

The process of writing this book was an opportunity for the three of us to change, to grow and to integrate parts of our experience of doing family and individual therapy. We came to understand explicitly how the communication skills we use in those contexts applied to the writing of this book together. We took three very different models of the world — three different types of backgrounds — and, finding a way to use our common skills to communicate with each other, we were able to put onto paper the knowledge we had gained. So we want to tell our readers some of the ways which we found delightful and useful to communicate, not only with families in the context of therapy, but also with each other in the process of writing this book. The very same patterns which we identify in this volume as patterns of effective communication with members of a family in the context of a therapy session are precisely the patterns of communication which we used to write this book together. We believe that our ability to be congruent in our communication is a skill we carry with us throughout our lives — both in our communication in therapy and in our other inter-personal relationships as well. It gives us great pleasure and is a continuing delight to find ways of being more effective in communicating with ourselves, with our colleagues in writing this book, and, hopefully, in communicating to you some of the excitement and joy we have experienced in the process of communication. For us, communication means experience — the ability to be in touch with what we are feeling, to see clearly what is available at a given point in time, and to hear with precision the sounds of life.

These skills, which we are constantly developing in ourselves, were the essential ingredients in the writing of this book. We want to emphasize that our desire in creating this book is to offer people-helpers some of the tools, patterns, ways of developing new choices with families which, up to this point in time, we have used only among ourselves. We invite and encourage each of you — as we will continue to do — to use these skills as an opportunity to find new possibilities for communication for yourselves and for the families with whom you work. We believe there are entire worlds of ways of being effective and creative — entirely new dimensions about human communication in our lives which we have yet to discover.

Deeply,

Richard Bandler
John Grinder
Virginia Satir

Preface

This book is about people who hurt and about the people who want to help them go beyond that hurt.

The world is full of good intentions and equally well populated with the evidence that these intentions do not always come to fruition. Parents want the best for their children, children for their parents, therapists for their clients, and clients for their therapists. How does it happen, then, that these very well-intentioned people have so many relationships of pain and trouble, when the opposite is what they are intending? Our belief is that something occurs which is outside of the awareness and control of either person — a missing piece. We believe that this missing piece can be added, learned about and fully used by everyone. This book is about our ideas of doing just that with families — helping them to find this missing piece for themselves.

It is hard for us to conceive how one can really experience himself as a responsible person without a thorough understanding of the difference between what people *intend* when they communicate and what the outcome of their communication *is*. We believe that all people, given the tools, not only want to, but will, learn and change. This is a normal direction of life asserting itself. We believe that all people have all of the skills they need; our job as family therapists is to make these skills accessible and useful for them. In this sense, no person is fragile. That is, everything which affects a human being or concerns him can be openly talked about, if it is presented to him in an acceptable way and at a time when he can hear it. In fact, for us, it amounts to a personal insult to behave toward another human being as though we could not openly acknowledge him and all of his parts. We believe that this is caring in its most exquisite sense. It is sometimes necessary for the therapist, when clearly allied with the growth goals of the one with whom he is working, to team up with the parts of that person desiring growth in such a way that the therapist becomes a tough leader in relation to the person's obstructive parts. It is difficult sometimes for a therapist to be present while another person is struggling, yet constructive struggle is the process by which we learn and grow. We believe that at any point in time every person is doing the best he can with the knowledge he has. We respect that, and at the same time we respect the wish and ability to change, and we are willing both to lead and to support the struggle to do so. In this sense, then, there need be no failures.

Our approach assumes that the therapist in his person is the chief tool for initiating change. Our view is that the therapist models that which he expects to change. We are speaking specifically of the *process* and not of the *content*. Our thrust is to change coping, which is a process, and, therefore, the therapist's use and teaching of process is a primary consideration. To be especially emphasized is the condition of the therapist's sensory channels: His ability to see, his ability to hear, his ability to feel, smell and taste need to be developed, operating, and clear. In our model it is essential that the therapist detect information and patterns of communication instead of deducing them. Furthermore, the therapist must be able to discriminate between inputs that trigger learnings and experiences from the past for himself and those which come entirely from the person with whom he is working. This means that the therapist is clearly able to distinguish between himself and his boundaries and those of the persons outside of him. It makes a great deal of difference in the therapeutic outcome whether the therapist talks and reacts to an extension of himself or to the person sitting in front of him. Keeping straight what's *you* and what's *me* is the thrust of all of this, and producing a meeting between the two is the goal.

It is our belief that at this point in time the evolvement of the condition of being human is only in its infancy. Therefore, it behooves all of us to become explorers and not judges; we see ourselves as making a contribution toward the further education of being human. As a matter of fact, we expect that we will come out of each of our experiences with other people a little changed. If we don't, then we feel that we will have fallen into the category of judging.

What we are presenting here is a model of the step-by-step process which fills in the missing pieces between what people intend in their communication and what the outcome of that communication actually is. Our method is to create new experiences instead of working to eliminate the old ones. Many therapeutic models of the past seem to have been built around the idea that there is an ideal person and, thus, the concepts were to be used as a way of altering the personality to fit the "ideal" mold. We believe that there is no universal model of a human being; we believe that each person has his own model of his own ideal. We are glad of it, and this uniqueness is what we strive for in our work. This is consistent with the biological fact that each human being is truly unique.

We want to emphasize that the model for family therapy which we present here is designed to create experience. It is our belief that much time and effort is wasted creating models which people then use to replace experience. The families — the people who come to therapists for help — are then squeezed into the categories contained in the model, rather than being sensed and responded to creatively. We offer our model as a way to assist you to fully participate in the moving experience of changing with families, participating in the process of growth, of creating experience, of the family's pain and the family's joy. Our model, essentially, is a way of helping people-helpers to tune themselves in to the ongoing processes for growth of the families with whom they are working — a way of seeing, hearing, feeling, sensing, experiencing and responding clearly and creatively to the process of communication and change in family therapy.

Our conclusion from our experience and from our observation of the people we have known is that they have learned five personal "unfreedoms" which fetter them and bind them and which are mistakenly called *civilized*. We will list them in their corrected form, which will include that which was corrected:

(1) The freedom to *see* and to *hear* what is NOW instead of what should be, could be, was, or will be.

(2) The freedom to *feel* what is felt NOW instead of what should be, could be, was, or will be.

(3) The freedom to *say* what is NOW instead of what should be, could be, was, or will be.

(4) The freedom to *reach out* for what you want instead of what you *should* want, not having to wait for someone to offer it to you.

(5) The freedom to *take risks* in your own behalf instead of only waiting for a change in the situation to make it possible for you to have what you want for yourself.

To summarize,
When I can *see* and *hear* what is here now, *feel* what I *feel* now;
Say what I *feel, think, hear, see* now;
When I can *reach out* for what I want now;
And can *take risks* in my own behalf now;
When I can *communicate* all of this congruently now;
And can get *feedback* creatively now;

Then I am in a position to cope inventively with the
   situation outside of myself and the life inside of
   me successfully —

NOW.

This book is our effort to translate people "unfreedoms" into freedoms.

PART I

Introduction

In the following pages we will present our particular view of the manifold and exciting field of family therapy. As with any complex area of human behavior, the ability of therapists to perform family therapy far outruns their ability to explicitly understand and communicate to others what they *specifically* do when they practice family therapy. The purpose of this book is to attempt to make understandable to the reader the patterns of which we have become aware in our practice of family therapy and to catch up the *theory* of family therapy with its *practice*. Specifically, by extracting the patterns of family therapy, we hope to accomplish several things: First, by forcing ourselves to become aware of the patterns of our own behavior in doing family therapy, we will become more systematic in our work and more effective as people-helpers, and, second, we will be able to more effectively communicate our experience to others

involved in family therapy so that a meaningful dialogue becomes possible among all of us as we help one
another to become more successful and dynamic in
our work.

The way that we hope to accomplish these goals is
by creating an explicit model or map for our behavior
in family therapy. By explicit model we simply mean a
guide for behavior which can be used by anyone wishing
to work as an effective family therapist. This guide for
doing family therapy will be explicit if it presents the
patterns necessary for a therapist to work in family
therapy effectively and creatively in a step-by-step
manner which makes it possible for the therapist to
learn and to use these patterns. As we understand it,
models or maps for behavior are not true or false, accurate or inaccurate, but, rather, they are to be judged as
useful or *not useful* for the purpose for which they were
intended. Since the model which we create here has as
its purpose to assist each of you in becoming a more
effective family therapist, we present it to you and invite
you to take the model, the patterns we identify here, and
to use them in your work in family therapy.

The first task which we need to accomplish is that
of finding some common experience with which each of
us, as family therapists, can identify. If we can succeed
in this, then we can all begin together the journey to a
better understanding of our work. If we can find this experience, then we can have a mutual reference point, or
point of departure, from which we can build the model
so that it will be useful for all of us. In a field as complex
as family therapy, there are so many places from which
we could start that it is difficult for us to choose among

them. However, we have decided to begin with the patterns of verbal communication — the patterns by which the therapist and the members of the family communicate with one another in words. This is not a judgment that words are more important than, or have some priority over, other forms of communication such as body movements, tone of voice, etc., but simply a place — a set of experiences — which we all share and from which we can begin.

In order to assist each of you as you read this book to connect the words before you on this page with the actual feelings, sights, sounds, smells, tastes — with the excitement of working with a real family in your experience — we will proceed by presenting excerpts from transcripts to illustrate the patterns in our experience which we wish to most vividly model. Finally, as we begin, we would like to remind you to identify the patterns from the transcripts in this first part of the book; this part is designed simply to give you practice in identifying the patterns. Once we have identified a pattern, we will not identify it again each time that it occurs, but, rather, we will continue to move on to other patterns. In Part II, we will sort these patterns into natural groups which will help you to organize your experience in family therapy. We suggest that you simply sit back, breathe comfortably and use your skills to connect the words before you with your own experience.

PATTERNS OF EFFECTIVE FAMILY THERAPY
LEVEL I

There are several important things which an effective family therapist assumes when he or she walks into
a session with a family. First, the fact that the family
has come to family therapy is a direct statement that
they have hopes that they can change. This is true in our
experience even when the family members are not aware
of it. In fact, even in the extreme case of court referrals,
the family has made a choice to come to therapy rather
than selecting jail. Their presence in therapy, then, is a
direct reflection of their hopes about continuing as a
family, and that they believe at some level that they are
capable of change.

Second, we assume, by the fact that the family is in
our presence for therapy, that they recognize at some
level that they need assistance in making those changes.
In our experience, we have found it useful to assume that
the family has the resources necessary to make those
changes, and our task, then, is to help them tap those resources. Thus, one of our major goals is to assist the
family members to recognize and accept the resources
already in the family system, although they may be presently unacknowledged and untapped. The therapist will
work to develop rapport and mutual trust with the
family as a necessary first step in making changes.
Without trust, no real risks will be attempted and no
real changes will occur.

Third, by accepting the particular therapist, the
family is accepting that person as a guide to lead them
in changing. The therapist serves as a model for the

family. More specifically, the therapist offers a model of openness — the freedom to select from what is available that which is relevant at the time and place for the therapist and for the family. This requires that the therapist be in touch with his own processes, as well as with the needs of the family. This modeling occurs not only at the conscious level but also at the subliminal level, i.e., the messages carried by the therapist's body posture, voice tone, etc., serve as a model for the family members.

We begin with an account of an opening session of family therapy. The therapist has just introduced himself and learned the names of the family members. Join us in a walk through the therapy session in which we will illuminate some of the ways by which the desired phenomena appear. We wish to point out to the reader that the following transcript is partial and fragmented. The quoted portion dealing with Dave is only a part of the full transcript. The therapist uses the same patterns and takes the same time and care with each family member in turn. To enable us to present these patterns in a clear way, we have left out sections of the transcripts.

Therapist: Well, I'm very pleased to be here with you this afternoon. I'm wondering what it is that each of you hopes to change by coming here to work together with me. I don't know whether the process which you went through in deciding to come here was easy or difficult for you, but I do know that your coming here is the first step in making those changes which each of you wants. (pause) Dave (addressing the father in the family), I'm curious whether you can shed some light on the hopes which you have for

yourself and your family. Can you tell me what you
hope, specifically, will change by your coming here?

Dave: Well ... I feel like we're just not pulling together
as a family ... like some things are missing ... I'm
just not sure. I can't get ahold of it — I can't get a
handle on it.

Therapist: Yes, Dave; can you tell me one thing that is
missing for you?

There are several important patterns in this short
transcript which emerge clearly. First, the therapist
assumes or presupposes that:

(1) There are things which the family wants to
change. *(... wondering what it is that each of
you hopes to change ... ; ... those changes
which each of you wants ... ; ... shed some
light on the hopes which you have ... ; ... what
you hope, specifically, will change ...)*

(2) The family went through the process of deciding
to come to therapy. *(... whether the process
which you went through in deciding to come
here was easy ...)*

(3) The process of change has already begun. *(...
your coming here is the first step in making
those changes ...)*

Notice that the therapist does not ask the family
members *if* they have hopes of being able to change;
rather, he presupposes that they *do*, and he asks, instead,

what are the specific changes which they desire. The family, thereby, comes to focus their attention on *what* changes and hopes rather than on *whether* changes and hopes exist. The therapist is systematic in the language forms he uses — specifically, he uses language assumptions *(presuppositions)*[1] as a tool in talking to the family in therapy. In other words, rather than using the language forms in column A, he uses those in column B:

A	B
Do you have hopes?	*What are your hopes?*
Did you go through a process of deciding to come here?	*Was your process of deciding to come here easy?*
Does each of you want changes?	*What, specifically, are those changes which each of you wants?*

By the skillful use of language assumptions (presuppositions), the therapist can assist the family in focusing upon the issues which are most important for achieving what they want in the therapeutic session.

We have found it to be very important in our experience to understand that the family therapist needs to make contact with each of the family members individually. The therapist must be careful not to assume that any one member of the family is a spokesperson for the rest of the family. The therapist makes a series of contracts for change — one for each family member. In this way, the therapist explicitly recognizes the integrity and independence of each member of the family. The basis of the art of family therapy is the therapist's ability to integrate the independent growth needs of each family member with the integrity of their family system. In exploring the desired changes with the individuals, the therapist makes skillful use of language assumptions (presuppositions). The specific language assumptions used by the therapist will be effective only to the extent that they are congruent with the growth needs of the family.

A second important pattern illustrated by the foregoing transcript is the delicate way in which the therapist begins the process of gathering information. There are several patterns which the therapist uses in the transcript. He begins with a statement about himself *(I'm very pleased to . . .).* Next, he uses a series of "questions" which aren't really questions in the usual sense. Notice, for example:

> *I'm wondering what it is that each of you . . .*
> *I don't know whether the process . . . was easy*
>   *or difficult . . .*
> *I'm curious whether you can shed some light . . .*

The particular language form used in this questioning is called *embedded questions.*[2] When questions are embedded as they are in the examples above, they do not demand an answer, yet they begin the process of bringing certain issues to the attention of the people listening — in this case, the issues concerning *which hopes* about *which changes* are held by each of the family members.

In addition, this form of questioning opens up the possibility for any one of the listeners to respond if he so chooses. In other words, it allows the listener the maximum number of choices about how and when he will respond. This seems to us to be particularly important in the initial stages of family therapy, when the therapist is gathering information. Finally, in conjunction with this pattern, the therapist pauses after he has presented several embedded questions, to allow any family member the space to exercise the choice of responding to the questions if he so chooses.

One of the choices which the therapist has when he receives no verbal response to the embedded questions is to select one of the family members and to identify him by name, requesting his response. Again, notice that, even after identifying the family member, the therapist is delicate in his questioning, using the embedded question first, *I'm curious whether you can* . . . . Furthermore, the therapist uses another important pattern as he becomes more direct in his attempt to gather information — the pattern of polite commands *(conversational postulates)*.[3] The therapist wants Dave, the father/husband, to respond to the embedded questions he has been asking. However, rather than directly stating a command — for example:

> *Dave, tell me, specifically, what you . . . ,*

the therapist asks Dave a question,

> *Can you tell me, specifically, what you . . .*

Again, later, after Dave has responded, the therapist uses the same form — the polite command *(conversational postulate)*:

> *Dave, can you tell me one thing that is missing for you?*

The important thing about this pattern is that, although what the therapist says has the *form* of a question which could be answered legitimately by a simple *yes* or *no*, it has the *force* of a command. Consider a common, everyday example: You and a friend are in the same room; the telephone rings, and your friend glances up at you and says,

> *Can you answer the phone?*

This sentence has the form of a simple question which requires only a *yes* or *no* answer, yet the typical response to it is for you to answer the phone. In other words, you will respond to this question as though your friend had made a direct request of you,

> *Answer the phone.*

The use of the yes/no form of a question in cases such as this is the polite way of making a direct request. Again, the therapist, by skillfully employing this pattern, leaves the family member maximum freedom to respond.

We return, now, to the transcript.

Therapist: Yes, Dave; can you tell me one thing that is
    missing for you?
Dave: I want some things for myself and I really feel
    that my family needs some things, too.
Therapist: Can you tell me what some of those things are?

The therapist has begun the task of coming to understand how Dave wants to change. He will repeat this
process with each of the family members. In order to be
effective in family therapy, the therapist needs to understand both what resources the family presently acknowl-
edges and uses, and also on what expectations the family
can agree — the desired state of the family system
toward which they agree to work. Each and every verbal
and non-verbal exchange with family members gives the
therapist information to understand the present state of
the family system and at the same time it gives the family members an opportunity to learn. By skillful communication, the therapist, from the very beginning, helps
the family members to develop a reachable goal for their
changes — the desired state. In this particular case, the
therapist is asking the male parent what he wants —
what changes in the family would be acceptable for him,
what he wants for himself and for his family. Dave
attempts to respond; he says,

> . . . *like some things are missing* . . .
> . . . *want some things for myself* . . .
> . . . *need some things, too* . . . .

The therapist's ears need to be tuned, to be open to detect
those parts of the verbal messages which do not pick out

specific parts of the speaker's world of experience. If the therapist is willing not to assume that he understands the generalities which he hears, he can make some meaning of them. Specifically, rather than assuming that his concept of the generalities being spoken is the same as the family member intends to communicate, the therapist can take the time and energy to determine more precisely the message from the person with whom he is working. The therapist may accomplish this in a graceful and sincere way by asking the other person to specify exactly to what he is referring when he uses those generalities.

It is important for us to emphasize that, while the therapist is using the pattern of language assumptions *(presuppositions)*, embedded questions and polite commands *(conversational postulates)* to gather information and to establish individual contracts for change with the family members, he is also offering information to them. The therapist gives his understanding of the messages presented by the family; for example, as he asks questions such as:

> *What specific changes do you hope for for yourself?*

he subtly presents his interpretation of what the family's presence for therapy means to him — namely, that their task is to make changes. This give-and-take process is an *example* of communication as well as *being* a communication in itself.

In each of Dave's responses, the therapist can identify a language form which fails to specify for the therapist some particular part of Dave's experience — the form: *some things*. This is an example of a common pattern — people coming to us for assistance often are not specific about what it is that they want or hope for. Our task, then, is to assist them in being specific. This is reflected in the words they use to communicate with others. When a part of a sentence picks out some specific portion of the listener's experience, then we say that that part has a *referential index*.[4] When a sentence part fails to pick out a specific part of the listener's experience, we say that it fails to have a referential index. Each time that Dave has responded, his sentence has included a part which failed to pick out a specific part of the therapist's experience *(to have a referential index)*. This is a signal to the therapist to request that the speaker supply a referential index:

> *Can you tell me one thing . . .*
> *Can you tell me what some of those things are . . .*

Here the therapist is systematically assisting Dave to identify what he wants. At the same time, the therapist is providing the family members with an effective way of communicating. When the therapist hears something which he is unable to connect with his own experience, rather than let unsuccessful communication slide by or pretend that he really understands or that he can read Dave's mind, he simply identifies the portion of the sentence which he could not understand and asks about it. Any assumptions need to be checked out. The therapist, by demanding clear communication, gives the family the message that he takes seriously both his ability to understand and their ability to communicate, and that he is interested in *really* understanding what they want.

Therapist: Can you tell me what some of those things are?
Dave: Well, I don't know.... I guess I've just lost touch....
Therapist: Lost touch with?
Dave: I don't know. ... . I'm not sure.
Therapist: Dave, what is it, specifically, that you don't know, that you're not sure of?
Dave: ... Well, I'm not sure anymore of what I want, for me or for my family. I'm a little bit scared.
Therapist: ... scared of?

The therapist is continuing to assist Dave in coming to understand what, specifically, it is that he wants for himself and his family. One of the most important patterns of which we are aware is the therapist's ability to sense what is missing in a family system. This capability to discern what is missing is critical in assisting the family in changing, and it applies at many different levels of behavior. For example, one thing which we, specifically, check for is the freedom of each family member to ask for what he wants. If that freedom is missing for any member of the family, then we work to find ways for him to gain that freedom. This is an example of something important which is missing at a high level of patterning. The process of identifying missing parts of experience and assisting the one with whom you are working in recovering them or completing imperfect experiences — of making things whole — is one of the most powerful interventions which we, as therapists, have available to us. The very process of making things whole, whether at a verbal or a non-verbal level, has a profound physical and neurological effect upon the person involved.

At the verbal level of patterning, Dave has produced a series of sentences, each of which has something missing. The therapist is responding systematically, first identifying that something is missing and then asking directly for it. For example, Dave says,

I've just lost touch.

As the therapist listens to this sentence, he tries to make sense out of it. He hears Dave describe his experience with the verb *lost touch*. In addition, he hears Dave say, specifically, that he (Dave) has *lost touch*. But, as the therapist attempts to understand what Dave is saying, he notices that Dave has failed to state with what *specifically* he has lost touch. In other words, the therapist understands that the descriptive verb *lose touch* is an expression of someone's losing touch with some*thing* or some*one*, and that what or whom it is is not stated — it is missing — or, in terms of a language description, it has been *deleted*.[5] We can represent this as follows: When the therapist (or any native speaker of American English) hears someone using the verb *lose touch*, he knows that it is a description of a process which has taken place between the person or thing doing the touching and the person or thing being touched:

LOSE TOUCH

person/thing   person/thing
touching   being touched

or

> LOSE TOUCH (person/thing touching,
> person/thing being touched).

The amazing thing is that, even when the sentence which the listener (in this case, the therapist) hears fails to include one or the other of these pieces, he knows by his intuitions about language that both of the pieces are implied. For example, when the therapist or any native speaker of English hears the following sentence, he understands that more is implied than is actually present in the sentence.

I lost touch ⟶ LOST TOUCH (I, someone/something)

One of the temptations for the therapist is to fill in his own understanding of what has been deleted, thereby losing the opportunity to learn what's missing for the family member.

Since the therapist can use his own language intuitions to determine whether anything is missing, he can listen and systematically respond, asking for the portions which are implied but not expressed. Extracting from the transcript, we have,

Dave	Missing Piece	Therapist
I don't know	. . . *know what* . . .	What don't you know?
I've just lost touch	. . . *lost touch with what* . . .	What have you lost touch with?
I don't know	. . . *know what* . . .	What don't you know?
I'm not sure	. . . *sure about* . . .	What aren't you sure about?
I'm a little bit scared	. . . *scared of* . . .	What are you scared of?

By listening carefully and making use of the intuitions he has about his language, the therapist can systematically assist Dave in understanding what he has deleted.

Therapist: Scared of?

Dave: Well, I know that Marcie (the mother/wife) is depending on me.

Therapist: How do you know that Marcie is depending on you, Dave?

Dave: Well, I know her pretty well; I just sense it.

Therapist: Yes; I understand that you know her pretty well, and what I'm trying to understand is how you communicate with her. Can you tell me how, specifically, you sensed just now that she was depending on you?

Dave: Sure; see the way that she's looking at me — that's how I know she's depending on me.

Words carry meanings. We need to understand that these words are idiosyncratic to the person using them, and there is no guarantee that the same meaning will be understood by the other person. So checking out is always necessary.

When each of us uses our language system to describe our experience, we select certain words to carry the meaning to the listener. For example, we use nouns to describe certain parts of our experience. As we mentioned previously, when we use nouns which have no referential index relative to a specific part of the listener's experience, we fail to communicate with as much clarity as is possible. Similarly, when we (albeit, unconsciously) select verbs to describe the processes or relationships which we experience, we have choices about how specific we will be, and, consequently, how clear our communication will be. For example, if I select the verb *kiss* to describe a process in my experience, I convey more information than if I select the verb *touch*, although both are accurate descriptions of my experience.

I kissed Judith   contrasted with   *I touched Judith*

The verb *kiss* conveys all of the meaning which the verb *touch* carries, with the additional specification that I touched Judith *with my lips*. In other words,

$$kiss \ = \ touch \ with \ lips$$

We can say, then, that the verb *kiss* (relative to the verb *touch*) is more specified; it gives the listener more information about the process being described. The verb *kiss* could, of course, be further particularized by specifying where the lips touched the person being kissed. This process we call *specifying verbs*.[6]

As the therapist goes about the task of assisting the family members in understanding what they seek, he sets a model for clear communication. In the verbal exchange, he can check the verbs which the family members use to describe their experience, requesting that they specify these process descriptions until he can make sense out of their narrations. Again, extracting from the transcript, we have,

Dave	Therapist
I know that Marcie is . . .	*How do you know that Marcie is . . .*
I just sense it . . .	*How, specifically, do you sense . . .*

By systematically insisting that he be able to understand the messages from individual family members, the therapist is setting an example for clear communication as well as teaching the family members specific ways to clear up their verbal communication.

Therapist: Dave, what are you aware of right now?

Dave: I feel kinda tight . . . stomach flipping around; you know . . . when Marcie looks at me that way, I feel kinda funny.

Therapist: Funny how?

Dave: You know, there's a lot of confusion . . . dependency makes me feel tight.

Therapist: You feel confused about what, Dave?

Dave: You know . . . dependency makes me feel confused . . .

Therapist: Whose depending on you makes you feel confused?

Human speech is one door to understanding between the speaker and the one to whom it is spoken. Understanding how human speech reflects this is an essential tool for therapists. We will, therefore, go into detail to show how this concept is illustrated in this interview.

There are several important patterns in this portion

of the transcript. First of all, Dave has begun to use a language pattern known as *nominalization*.[7] Nominalization is the name of the linguistic process by which people represent active portions of their experience by words which are usually used to represent the more static portions of their experience. Nouns are usually used to represent these more inert portions of our experience — *chair, table, stove, mirror*, etc. — while verbs are normally used to represent the more dynamic parts of our experience — *running, jumping, watching, listening*, etc. However, through the language process of nominalization, we represent the active portions of our experience in a static way. For example, in the following two sentences, both of the words in italic seem to function as nouns.

> I see *cats*.
> I see *frustration*.

The word *cats* serves to separate from the world of experience a particular type of animal, while the word *frustration* represents something quite different. *Frustration* is associated with the verb *frustrate* which sounds and looks very much like it and has a similar meaning. The verb *frustrate* is the name of a process by which *someone/something* is frustrating *someone*. Using the kind of visual representation we developed previously in our discussion of the linguistic process of deletion, we have,

> *FRUSTRATE (something/someone doing the*
> *frustrating, someone being frustrated)*

So, when the therapist (or any native speaker of English) hears the sentence,

I see frustration.

he can, by checking his intuitions about the meaning, discover that there is more implied by the sentence than actually appears on the surface. Specifically, we have,

I see frustration ⟶ *SEE (I, FRUSTRATE [someone/ something, someone])*

In the example we are presenting, the linguistic process of using a noun for a verb description (the process of nominalization) also includes the process of deleting the information associated with the original verb description.

In the transcript, Dave uses two nominalizations, *confusion* and *dependency*. As the therapist continues to try to comprehend the present family system and what its members want, he encounters these nominalizations. As is typical of nominalizations, so much of the material associated with the verb of process representation has been deleted that the therapist cannot fully understand Dave's communication. The following exchanges then occur:

Dave	Therapist
A lot of confusion . . .	*You feel confused about what?*
Dependency makes me . . .	*Whose depending on you makes . . .*

Notice that the therapist is systematic in his responses; he identifies the nominalizations, and

    (a) Turns the noun word back into a verb word:

        confusion ⟶ feel confused

        dependency ⟶ depending

    (b) Assumes that Dave is one of the deleted parts of the nominalization:

        a lot of confusion ⟶ you *feel confused about what?*

        dependency makes ⟶ *whose depending on* you *makes . . .*

    (c) Asks for the other part of the nominalization which has been deleted:

        a lot of confusion ⟶ *you feel confused about* what?

        dependency makes ⟶ whose *depending on you makes . . .*

There are two ways which we have found very useful in our work to systematically identify and challenge nominalizations in the communications of family members in the context of family therapy. First, people are unable to cope when they represent *processes* in their experience as *events*, static and fixed, having deleted most of the information about the parts which went to make up that process. If the missing something which they want in their lives is represented as a *process* with the parts of that process identified, then there is a possibility for them to act to influence and change the process to get what they want. Understanding how they arrived at the place in their lives where they are now helps them to identify the next step toward getting what they want for themselves. If, however, the thing they want is represented as an *event* with most of the pieces missing, they have little hope of influencing and changing it. They, literally, are victims of their representation. When the nominalizations are converted into process representations and the pieces of the process are identified, coping becomes possible. Dave feels confused about what he is to do when Marcie looks at him in a certain way. Understanding the *specific process* by which "a lot of confusion" is created is an important first step in *changing* it.

Secondly, when a family comes to us for assistance, they are usually able to agree that they seek some nominalization such as *love, warmth, support, respect, comfort*, etc., for themselves. However, unless the therapist is alert to connect these words with experience (de-nominalize these nominalizations), filling in the deletions, etc., for each of the family members, there is little hope that the individuals will be satisfied. In other words, since each family member regards a different experience as *love, warmth*, etc., these words connect with experience (de-nominalize nominalizations) differently for each of them. What one of them regards as warmth another may consider smothering. By systematically connecting words with specific experiences (de-nominalizing) with each of the family members, the therapist can identify the experience or set of experiences which all of the family members will be able to accept as fulfilling their desires and hopes for themselves as individuals and as a family. By de-nominalizing, the therapist establishes the experiences which will be satisfying for the family and which he can then work with them to create. These experiences constitute the *desired state* of the family system; they allow the therapist to compare what the family resources are at this point in time with what they will need to create in order to reach the state they agree upon (through the process of de-nominalization) as being appealing to them. By this process, a direction is established for the therapist and the family members to organize the experience of family therapy.

Many times in our experience, using the verbal techniques of de-nominalization, a family member will begin with one nominalization and, in the process of connecting it with specific experiences, will supply another nominalization as one of the missing pieces. For example,

Dave: You know, there's a lot of confusion . . .
Therapist: You feel confused about what, Dave?
Dave: Dependency makes me feel confused . . .

Notice what has happened here: Dave uses a nominalization, *confusion,* which is somehow connected with a part of Dave's experience which he wants to change. The therapist applies the verbal de-nominalization. Dave responds by supplying one of the missing pieces; however, the missing piece which he provides is, itself, a nominalization. The therapist alertly applies the verbal de-nominalization again:

Therapist: Whose depending on you makes you feel confused, Dave?

This kind of cycle is one which we find frequently in our family therapy work. By systematically applying the verbal de-nominalization technique to each nominalization, the therapist succeeds in assisting the family member in identifying by exactly what process he is perceiving or failing to perceive what he is experiencing. This process of cyclic de-nominalization (by tying the word description to things which are in the "real" world of experience) allows both the therapist and the family members to understand the specific experiences which they can create together to continue the process of change and growth.

A second important pattern in this portion of the transcript is contained in the statements which Dave makes:

> *Dependency makes me feel tight . . .*
> *Dependency makes me feel confused . . .*

These two sentences have the same form — each of them claims that there is something *(dependency)* outside of the person involved in the description which causes that person to experience a certain feeling. In other words, each of these sentences claims that there is a Cause-Effect relationship over which the person involved has no control and which, literally, *makes* him have a certain experience.

Linguists have identified a certain class of sentences such as:

> *Max makes Sue weigh 357 pounds on Tuesdays.*

and

> *Mildred forces Tom to be 8 feet tall on Saturdays.*

as *semantically ill-formed.*[8] That is, sentences of this class make claims which are at odds with our usual understanding of the way the world operates. Specifically, these sentences claim that one person is causing another person to have a certain experience. However, since the experience which the sentences claim the second person is having is an experience which most of us consider to be beyond the conscious control of human beings, the sentences, literally, make no sense. In other words, since Sue (or anyone else) cannot control what she weighs on a certain day of the week, it makes no sense to claim that Max is causing her to control her weight in that way.

Within the context of therapy, we have found an extension of this linguistic class very useful. Specifically, any sentence such as:

> *He makes me sad.*

is called *Cause-Effect semantically ill-formed.*[9] Several examples may help to identify the pattern in your experience:

> *She makes me really mad.*

> *He really makes her sad.*
> *Walking along the beach makes me feel*
> *refreshed.*

We understand that these sentences may be a valid description of a person's experience. However, what we are saying is that the Cause-Effect relationship which each of these sentences seems to require is not necessary. We have determined in working with people in therapy that, all too frequently, their pain and lack of freedom and choice are connected with parts of their experience which they represent in the Cause-Effect semantically ill-formed pattern we have just identified. This, typically, takes the form:

> *This caused that.*
> *I am helpless.*
> *It is final.*

We have found it useful in our work to assist people in having a choice about whether a particular movement, act, smile, word, etc., from someone else necessarily *has* to have the effect on them that they claim. Typically, people who do not have such choices experience little or no control and responsibility over their own lives. Specifically, as therapists we have found that we can effectively assist clients in coming to have these choices by asking them to describe in detail the process by which someone *causes* them to feel or sense what they are experiencing. The process of assisting the one with whom we are working in understanding the specific way in which he fails to have a choice in his verbal and non-verbal communication with others typically involves the linguistic patterns we have already presented, especially denominalization and the specification of verbs. We have found this pattern to be a very useful model.

We return, now, to the transcript.

Dave: You know, dependency makes me feel confused.

Therapist: Hold on a minute, Dave; let me see if I understand this. When you see Marcie look at you in a certain way, you know that she's depending on you and you feel tight, is that right, Dave?

Dave: Yeah, that's right. I never have been able to get a handle on it; you know, altogether, like I felt when you just said it now.

Therapist: Let's check this out, Dave. (turning to Marcie, the wife/mother in the family) Marcie, you heard what Dave said about knowing that you're depending on him when you look at him in a certain way, and I'm wondering whether . . .

Dave: (interrupting) Yeah, you know, Marcie, like right now, when your eyes get narrow and you lean forward, I know that you're unhappy with me, and . . .

Therapist: Wait, Dave. (turning again to Marcie) Marcie, are you unhappy with Dave right now?

Marcie: No, I'm trying to understand what's going on here, and . . .

One of the ways in which people in families create pain and unhappiness for themselves is by assuming that they can come to know the thoughts and feelings of another person without that other person's directly communicating those thoughts and feelings. We call this *Mind Reading semantic ill-formedness*.[10] Mind Reading occurs in any situation in which one person claims to know the inner experience of another without a direct communication of the second person's experience. Frequently, this takes the form of:

> *If you loved me, you would know without my telling you.*

Extracting from the transcript, we have:

Dave	Therapist's Response
I know that Marcie is depending upon me.	*How do you know that Marcie is . . .*
I know that you're unhappy with me.	*How do you know, specifically, that . . .*

In these two exchanges, we can identify both the Mind-Reading pattern and one of the ways in which the therapist can usefully challenge this process by specifically asking for a detailed description of the process by which the person (Dave, in this case) obtained the information he claims to have. This process (Mind Reading) is one of the most tragic ways by which well-intentioned people in a family can distort their communication and cause pain. We realize that it is possible to understand a great deal about the inner experience of another person without his having to describe it in detail in words. One of the skills which we continue to sharpen in our work as therapists is the ability to identify and understand another person's experience through the analogue (non-verbal) messages which they present to us. The tone of voice, the posture, movements of the hands and feet, the tempo of speech — are all important messages which we each utilize in our work. We accept for ourselves the rule of explicitly checking our comprehension of non-verbal messages rather than basing further communication upon our assumed understanding of those messages. What we have noticed time and again is that, under stress, people tend to hallucinate the inner experience of others and to act upon those hallucinations without checking first to find out if they match the actual experience of the other person. Once this process of Mind Reading without checking begins, clear communication becomes difficult and finally collapses, and we see a family in pain. In our experience, the therapist's ability to identify and effectively challenge the Mind-Reading pattern is one of the most important interventions in assisting a family to move from a rigid, closed system to one which allows freedom to grow and change.

Closely associated with the general pattern of Mind Reading is another important pattern, that of *Complex Equivalence*[11] — the names which people attach to their experience.

Therapist	Dave
Tell me, specifically, how you sensed just now that she was depending upon you.	*Sure; see the way she's looking at me . . . that's how I know that she's depending upon me.*

I'm wondering whether   *When your eyes get narrow*
. . .   *and you lean forward, I*
                         know that you're unhappy
                         with me.

Dave is presenting us with an excellent illustration of the way in which people calibrate their experience. Dave has decided that, whenever he sees Marcie looking at him in a certain way (not specified), she is depending upon him; she is experiencing an inner state which he labels "dependency." In the second example, Dave has decided that, whenever Marcie narrows her eyes and leans forward, she is unhappy with him. What is common to both instances is that Dave has equated a piece of Marcie's observable behavior with her total communication and then has labeled it an inner experience.

Examples of Complex Equivalence

Observable Behavior		Inner Experience
Marcie looks a certain way.	=	*Marcie is depending upon Dave.*
Marcie narrows her eyes and leans forward.	=	*Marcie is unhappy with Dave.*

What we are illustrating here is that people cause themselves pain and difficulty by attaching a word (label) to some part of their experience and mistaking the label for the experience. One powerful phenomenon we have seen in our work is the fact that people pay particular attention to different portions of their experience and, subsequently, may come to attach the same label to a very different experience. For example, for people who use their visual skills most extensively, the word *respect* will, typically, have something to do with eye contact, while people who emphasize body sensations (kinesthetic representational system) will pay more attention to the way others touch them. By this process, people may use the same word to describe very different experiences. We call this process *Complex Equivalence* (the experiences which the words represent) and, typically, it may be quite diverse for different people. In other words, instead of using feedback (for example, *asking* Marcie what was going on), Dave has calibrated his experience so that, whenever he detects certain movements by Marcie, he "knows" what she is experiencing. Notice that the therapist makes two different types of responses to Dave's Mind-Reading—Complex-Equivalence statements. First, the therapist re-states the claim that Dave has made about Mind Reading and the specific Complex Equivalence which he uses. This serves two purposes: The therapist checks to make sure that he understands the Mind-Reading process which Dave is presenting; at the same time, the therapist's re-statement allows Dave to hear a complete description of the process. In fact, those with whom we work frequently will laugh out loud when the contention which they have just made is repeated to them, recognizing that the connection claimed is spurious. For others, the therapist's re-statement allows them to fully understand the process for the first time. Dave's response is a good example of this:

I never have been able to get a handle on it; you

> *know, altogether, like I felt when you just*
> *said it now . . .*

The second response which the therapist makes is
to challenge the Mind-Reading—Complex-Equivalence pattern in the family by turning to the other family member
involved — in this case, Marcie — and asking her to state
whether or not Dave's Mind Reading—Complex Equivalence was accurate. As the transcript shows, Dave was
hallucinating. (We use this word [hallucinate] when we
are referring to ideas which are "made up" when factual
data are not available. Our brain must make *something*
from everything. We do not consider it pathological in
this context, only descriptive.) Marcie was not, in fact,
unhappy with him at that point in time. In our experience in therapy, so much of the pain experienced by
members of a family is connected with calibrated communication, communication based upon Mind Reading
and Complex Equivalence. This makes the therapist's
ability to detect and effectively challenge these patterns
extremely important.

Marcie: No, I'm trying to understand what's going on
here, and, . . .
Therapist: Thank you, Marcie. (turning back to Dave)
Dave, I want you to try something new for yourself
and Marcie. Are you willing to try something new,
Dave?
Dave: Well, yeah, OK . . . I'll try. What is it?
Therapist: Dave, I want you to look directly at Marcie
and tell her how you're feeling right now, and as
you do . . .

Dave: (interrupting) Oh, no; I'd really like to, but I just can't.

Therapist: You can't, Dave? What stops you?

Dave: Huh? What stops me?

Therapist: Yes, Dave, what stops you from looking directly at Marcie while you tell her what you are feeling?

Dave: I don't know ... I really don't know. I just can't.

Therapist: Dave, could you tell me what would happen if you did this?

Dave: What would happen? I don't know ...

Therapist: Guess, Dave!

In this portion of the transcript, the therapist has made a request to Dave to try something new, something which runs counter to the calibrated communication, involving the Mind Reading and Complex Equivalence, which is going on between him and Marcie. Dave's response is to state that it is impossible to do what the therapist has asked: *I just can't.* Now, the therapist knows from his own experience — of looking directly at Marcie when he communicates with her — that looking directly at her when speaking to her is possible for *him.* Therefore, if Dave thinks that this is impossible, then his claim is a signal that he has been asked to perform an act which is outside of his model of the world and, more specifically, outside of his model of what is possible *for him with Marcie.* One of the patterns which has assisted us most in organizing our experiences in family therapy is our ability to detect the limits of the family members' models of the world — what acts are, literally, beyond the limits which they allow themselves. In natural language systems (verbal), there are a small number of expressions which logicians call *modal operators*[12] of possibility and necessity. These are words and phrases which *specifically* identify the limits of the speaker's model of the world. By identifying these limits, we are able to help the person involved to extend his model to include what he wants for himself and his family, to turn into a *choice* something which he has regarded as inevitable. In the following exchange between Dave and the therapist,

Modal Operators (Dave)	Therapist's Response
But I just can't . . .	*What stops you?*
I just can't . . .	*What would happen if you did?*

the two responses by the therapist assist Dave in extending the limits of his model to continue the process of change toward what he wants for himself and Marcie.

Next, we list some of the most common words and phrases in the English language which identify limits in a person's model and, opposite them, the two verbal challenges we have found most effective in helping to change these limits.

Modal Operators of Possibility	Therapist's Challenges
unable to, can't, impossible, must not, no way	*What stops you?*

Modal Operators of Necessity	Therapist's Challenges
have to, necessary, must, no choice, forced to	*What would happen if you did?*

The therapist's challenges to these cue words and phrases, which identify the limits of the family's model of what is possible for them, have, in our experience, been extremely effective in assisting in the process of change.

Closely associated with modal operators is the type of exchange illustrated by the following part of the transcript:

Dave: Oh, no; I'd really like to, but I just can't.
Therapist: What stops you?
Dave: I really don't know . . . I just can't.
Therapist: Dave, what would happen if you did?
Dave: I really don't know.
Therapist: Guess, Dave!

Often, when using verbal patterns to assist the family members in changing, we have received the reply, *I don't know.* We often ask them to guess. We have found that asking people to guess relieves them of the pressure to know accurately, and, therefore, they can come up with more relevant material. By responding with a congruent *guess*, time and again we have enabled family members to express something important about what stops them from getting something they want for themselves. When requested to guess when he claims not to know the answer to some question, the family member invariably produces an answer. The answer can come from only one place, his model of the world. Thus, his answer tells us a great deal about how he organizes his experience, what resources are available to him, what limits he accepts, etc.

We continue now with the transcript. Essentially, in the section we skip, the therapist continued to work with Dave, assisting him in understanding just what it is that he wants for himself and for his family. The therapist accomplished this, primarily, by insuring that he understands what Dave is telling him; he insists that Dave communicate in language without nominalizations, deletions, relatively unspecified verbs, or nouns without referential indices. We begin the transcript again just after the therapist has turned his attention to Marcie, the mother/wife member of the family.

Therapist: Well, Marcie, you have had an opportunity to listen and watch as I worked with Dave, your husband. I'm wondering what you were aware of as you did this. Would you be willing to say?

Marcie: Sure; I think that I see pretty clearly what you are trying to do. You know — I have eyes, and I'm no dummy; I get the picture.

Therapist: What *specifically* did you see, Marcie?

The therapist is illustrating a very important principle here: He has directed his verbal communication to one of the family members. During this period, the other members of the family have had an opportunity to observe and to listen to the process of communication between the therapist and Dave. The therapist now asks Marcie to comment on her experience of the exchange between Dave and the therapist. By requesting her comments (by using embedded questions and polite commands [conversational postulates]), the therapist accomplishes several things:

(a) He gives each member of the family the message that, not only does he accept comments on his behavior and the ongoing process of communication, but he, in fact, encourages them, that he takes seriously their ability to understand and make sense out of their experience and is interested in knowing what that experience is to them.

(b) He requests that another member of the family present him with the results of her ability to make sense out of a complex piece of family interaction.

The therapist pointedly requests that Marcie present her learnings and understanding of the interaction between Dave and himself. This is one important way that the therapist may explicitly present the message that, although he has been directing his verbal communication to Dave, all of the family members are involved at the same time; they are all participants in the ongoing process of communication. Secondly, when the therapist encourages Marcie to comment about her experience of the Dave-therapist interaction, he is asking her to repeat a learning experience with which we are all familiar. As children, each of us learned a great deal of what we understand about the world by observing and listening to our parents and other adults communicate. This time, the context openly invites people to "listen in," in contrast to much of childhood's experience in which this was tacitly forbidden. By explicitly repeating this situation, the therapist provides an opportunity for Marcie to up-date her old learnings — her understandings from her original family system.

Each of us organizes and represents our experiences of the world and each other differently, in ways which are unique to each of us. My experience of the "same world" will differ from yours in some ways. Through our initial genetic heritage and from our extensive experience in coping and living, each of us has created a map or model of the world which we use to guide our behavior. We do not experience the world directly but rather through the models of the world which we have developed to help us organize our ongoing experience. The means by which we develop and elaborate our models of the world are the three universals of human modeling — deletion, distortion and generalization.[13] When we pay attention only to selected portions of our environment and ignore others, we are using the modeling principle of *deletion*. When we represent to ourselves a two-dimensional object, we are *distorting*. When we approach a door which we have never seen before, reach out and grasp the door handle, turn it and pull open the door without any conscious decision about the process, we are making use of the modeling principle of *generalization* — that is, in our previous experience, whenever we saw and felt a door with a handle, we succeeded in opening the door by grasping the handle, turning it and pulling it, so we automatically generalize to the new experience — the new door. Over our years of experience, we have each developed strategies (mostly unconsciously) for modeling our experience. By asking Marcie to comment on what she was aware of during the exchange between himself and Dave, the therapist has an opportunity to compare *his* awareness of the model he created with Marcie's impressions. Specifically, the therapist can learn, by listening to Marcie's response, which of the different ways of representing her experience she values most highly — that is, what Marcie's most used *representational system*[14] is. How can the therapist specifically determine this from the response he receives from Marcie? Below, we list the descriptive verbs and other parts of the sentences which Marcie uses which are most closely associated with verb or process descriptions:

Marcie

think	*see clearly*	trying	do	*eyes*	get *picture*

We will refer to these words as process words *(predicates)* which, roughly, include *verbs, adverbs, adjectives,* and *nominalizations.* Of the eight predicates used by Marcie in this first communication, four are words which presuppose a visual representation of Marcie's experience. The other four predicates are unspecified with respect to the kind of representation they indicate. For example, a person can try or do something using *sounds* (an *auditory* representation) or *feelings* (a *kinesthetic* representation), etc. One way to understand an important type of patterning in Marcie's communication and in her ability to make sense out of (or *model*) her experience is to notice that her choice of predicates confirms that the primary way by which she creates a representation of her experience is by creating pictures or images of it. In the terms we are developing here for our family therapy model, Marcie's choice of predicates reveals that her most used representational system is visual. Next, we list some of the predicates which Dave used to express himself earlier in the transcript.

Dave				
feel	*pulling*	sure	*get a hold of*	*get a handle on*
want	*feel*	need	know	*lost touch* ...

Of the ten predicates listed above used by Dave, more than half of them presuppose a kinesthetic representational system — that is, Dave organizes his experience, his model of the world, by feelings. Thus, Dave's most used representational system is kinesthetic. The remaining predicates used by Dave are consistent with this statement, as they are unspecified with respect to representational system.

Knowing a person's most used representational system is, in our experience, a very useful piece of information. One way in which we have found this useful is in our ability to establish effective communication. As therapists, if we can be sensitive to the most used representational system of the person with whom we are working, we then have the choice of translating our communication into his system. Thus, he comes to trust us as we demonstrate that we understand his ongoing experience by, for example, changing our predicates to match his.

Being explicit about how the other person organizes his or her experience of the world allows us to avoid some of the typical "resistant client—frustrated therapist" patterns such as those described in Part I, *The Structure of Magic, II*, Grinder and Bandler:

> We have in past years (during in-service training seminars) noticed therapists who asked questions of the people they worked with with no knowledge of representational systems used. They typically use only predicates of their own most highly valued representational systems. This is an example:

> > *Visual Person:* My husband just doesn't see me as a valuable person.
> > *Therapist:* How do you feel about that?
> > *Visual Person:* What?
> > *Therapist:* How do you feel about your husband's not feeling that you're a person?

> This session went around and around until the therapist came out and said to the authors:

> > *I* feel *frustrated; this woman is just giving me a* hard *time. She's resisting everything I do.*

> We have heard and seen many long, valuable hours wasted in this form of miscommunication by therapists with the people they work with. . . . The therapist in the above transcript was really

trying to help and the person with him was really trying to cooperate but without either of them having a sensitivity to representational systems. Communication between people under these conditions is usually haphazard and tedious. The result is often name calling when a person attempts to communicate with someone who uses different predicates.

Typically, kinesthetics complain that auditory and visual people are insensitive. Visuals complain the auditories don't pay attention to them because they don't make eye contact during the conversation. Auditory people complain that kinesthetics don't listen, etc. The outcome is usually that one group comes to consider the other as deliberately bad or mischievous or pathological.

The point we are illustrating here is that one of the most powerful skills we, as therapists, can develop is the ability to be sensitive to representational systems. For change to occur, for the persons with whom we are working to be willing to take risks, for them to come to trust us as guides for change, they must be convinced that we understand their experience and can communicate with them about it. In other words, we accept as our responsibility as people-helpers the task of making contact with the persons we are trying to help. Once we have made contact — by matching representational systems, for example — we can assist them in expanding their choices about representing their experience and communicating about it. This second step — that of leading the individual toward new dimensions of experience — is very important. So often, in our experience, family members have "specialized" — one paying primary attention to the visual representation of experience, another to the kinesthetic portion of experience, etc.

For example, we discover from the transcript that *Dave's* primary representational system is *kinesthetic*, while *Marcie's* is *visual*. Once we have made contact, we work to assist Dave in developing his ability to explore the *visual* dimensions of his experience and to assist Marcie in getting in touch with *body sensations*.[15] There are two important results of this:

(a) Dave and Marcie learn to communicate effectively with one another.

(b) Each of them expands his/her choices about representing and communicating their experiences, thus becoming more developed human beings — more whole, more able to express and use their human potential.

Within the context of family therapy, by identifying each family member's most used representational system, the therapist learns what portions of the ongoing family experience is most available to each person there. Understanding this allows the therapist to know where, in the communication patterns of the family, to look for faulty communication, where the family members fail to communicate what they intend. For example, if one family member is primarily visual and another auditory, the family therapist will be alert to note how they communicate, how they give each other feedback. Under stress particularly, each of us tends to depend only upon our primary representational system. We come to accept a *part* of our experience as an equivalent for the *whole* — accepting, for example, only what we *see* as equivalent to what is totally available not only through our eyes but also through our *skin*, our *ears*, etc. This explains the close connection between representational systems and the kinds of Mind Reading and Complex Equivalences developed by family members.

At this point in the presentation of the patterns which we have identified as useful in organizing our experience in therapy, we are going to shift the way in which we present the transcript. We have identified the most important of the verbal patterns which are in our family therapy model and, with the presentation of the principle of representational systems, we have begun to move to the next level of patterns. Verbal communications and your ability to hear the distinctions which we have presented are very useful portions of an effective model for family therapy. These verbal patterns and your ability to respond systematically to them, however, constitute only a portion of the complete model. In the presentation of the transcript up to this point, we have confined ourselves to reporting the verbal patterns. In this way, we hoped to find a common reference point from which each of you could connect what we are describing with words here in this book with your own experience in therapy. We hoped that, by finding this common reference point, you would be able to utilize, immediately and dynamically in your work, the patterns which we have identified.

Now we move on to patterns at the next level of experience, patterns which have as one of their parts the verbal patterns which we have just identified.

PATTERNS OF EFFECTIVE FAMILY THERAPY
LEVEL II

Each of us, as a human being, has many choices about the way in which we present ourselves — the way by which we communicate. Most of the time, as we meet and separate and meet again, we do not make conscious decisions about the way we communicate. Normally, for example, we do not *consciously* select the specific words and even less frequently do we consciously select the syntactic form of the sentences with which we communicate verbally. Yet, even at this level of communication patterning, the *unconscious* choices which we make are systematic and reveal a great deal about the ways in which we organize our experience, grow and change. This, in fact, is one way to understand the verbal patterns which we have identified in Level I. These patterns of choice made by the persons with whom we are working in therapy about the form of the sentences which they use to present themselves are ways in which the therapist can come to quickly and efficiently understand their model of the world, the way in which they organize their experience.

Verbal communication constitutes only a portion of the complex process of communication which goes on between people. At the same time that people are presenting one another with words and the formal verbal patterns we have identified, they are also holding some portions of their body in a certain posture; they are moving their hands and feet, their arms and legs with smooth or erratic, rhythmic or arhythmic motions; they are speaking with a tone of voice which is melodic, raspy, lilting, or grating; they are speaking at a constant tempo, or speeding up and slowing down; they are moving their eyes in a rapidly shifting scan, or maintaining a fixed stare, with their eyes focused or unfocused; they are altering the rhythm of their breathing, etc. Each of these movements, gestures, tones, etc., are choices which they make, usually at the unconscious level, about the way they present themselves, the way they communicate. Each of these is, in fact, a message about their ongoing experience, about the way they organize their world, of what they are most acutely aware. Just as with the verbal patterns, when each of the patterns, once detected by the therapist, could be used by him for a specific, effective therapeutic intervention, here also, in the case of the messages carried by the person's voice, body movements, etc., the therapist can train himself to identify patterns and to intervene to assist the person to grow and change.

One of the most useful ways of proceeding in this complex area, in our experience, is for therapists to educate themselves to identify patterns of *congruity* and *incongruity*. When a person is communicating congruently, all of the messages which he conveys match — they are consistent, they fit with one another. Incongruent communication is presented to us when the other person sends out messages with his body, with his voice tonality, with the words he uses, which do not match. In order to learn to detect this mishmash and to respond creatively to it, either in therapy or in the day-to-day contact we have with one another, we must have clear, open channels for receiving and organizing *all* of this information. There is no substitute for the therapist's ability to *see*, to *hear*, and to *feel*. In order to distinguish congruent from incongruent communication, the therapist must clear his input channels. By failing to clear the channels he runs the risk of either being preoccupied and missing the other person's messages or of hallucinating spurious messages instead of being receptive to what's actually being presented. When a therapist fails to clear all of his senses, he usually succeeds only in Mind Reading rather than in identifying and responding creatively to the messages from the person with whom he is working.

Each of us has a nervous system, a personal history, and a view or model of the world which are unique to us. When we meet another person and communicate carefully, we are sensitive to the other individual in hopes of truly making contact and learning to appreciate his uniqueness, even as we, ourselves, change and grow from our experience of the differences between us. Much of our education is directed toward insuring that the verbal language which we share with other speakers (English, for this book) overlaps enough to enable us to make contact. This gives the people in the same language/culture group a basis for communication. In the case of the languages of the body, tonality, etc., almost no formal education is given to us; in fact, little is known about these languages. Yet, these non-verbal messages constitute the bulk of the information which is communicated by human beings.

One of the ways in which each of you can become more sensitive to the variances from person to person in the non-verbal language which carries so much of our communication is to consider the differences in gestural and body language from culture to culture. In some cultures (Italian, for example), holding the hand palm-up at about chin level, extended in front of you, and opening and closing the hand is a way of signaling *goodbye*, while, in our culture, this gesture means something close to *come here*. It is also true in our experience that within cultures there are many differences in the meaning of the elements of non-verbal language. The furrowed brow for one person may be a signal of anger and displeasure while, for another person, it may simply signal concentration. Or again, shifting your gaze from the face of the person to whom you're speaking, just after hearing a question and prior to responding, is a signal in the behavior of one person roughly equivalent to *I'm uncomfortable and don't want to respond*, while, in another person, it is simply a way of cueing himself (specifically, of making a picture which will serve as the basis of the response) to respond appropriately. Translating it into words, it means (approximately), *I'm organizing my experience with pictures and will respond in a moment*. Each of the body movements, postures, tonalities, etc., which we employ in the non-verbal languages we use to communicate is the result of our own personal history, our own nervous system; few, if any, of these are conscious; few, if any, of these are standardized, either within our culture or across cultures. The point we are making here is that, while the bulk of communication between people is non-verbal, little of it is calibrated, and there is a great deal of room for miscommunication, especially in the Mind-Reading and Complex-Equivalence phenomena we have previously identified.

One very general overview of the process of communication which we have found useful in organizing our experience is that each communication — composed of the specific body posture, movement, voice tone and tempo, the words, and the sentence syntax — can be understood to be a comment on three areas of the on-going experience:

The communicator, *Self;*
The person to whom the communication is addressed, the *Other;* and
The *Context*.

We represent this visually by the symbol:

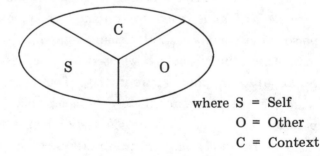

where S = Self
O = Other
C = Context

We have found it useful to check a person's communication for his ability to be aware of and communicate about each of these dimensions. If, for example, a person is unable, at a given point in time, to be aware of and to represent to himself and to others (communicate) each of these parts of human experience, then this present inability is connected with the difficulties in his life which brought him to us for therapy. Thus, it indicates to us where we may choose to intervene to assist him in developing his ability to experience and make sense out of each of these parts of human experience, thereby creating more choices for himself. Notice that the same modeling processes detailed in the patterns of verbal communication in Level I of this part of the book also occur here at this higher level of patterning. When a family member says to us,

> *I'm scared.*

we understand that he has deleted (linguistically) a portion of his experience; specifically, *who* or *what* is scaring him. When a family member is unable to be aware of and communicate about his own feelings and thoughts, or his experience of another family member with whom he is communicating, or the context in which the communication takes place, he is deleting (behaviorally) a portion of his experience and also a portion of his potential as a human being. In our experience, the process of restoring this deletion will be a very powerful learning experience for the individual, and it will assist him in having more choices in his life.

One of us [Virginia Satir] has identified four communication categories or stances which people adopt under stress. Each of these Satir categories is characterized by a particular body posture, set of gestures, accompanying body sensations, and syntax. Each is a caricature:

Satir Category	Caricature of
Placating	*Service*
Blaming	*Power*
Super-Reasonable	*Intellect*
Irrelevant	*Spontaneity*

(1) Placater

Words — agree — ("Whatever you want is okay. I am just here to make you happy.")

Body — placates — ("I am helpless.")

Insides — ("I feel like a nothing; without him I am dead. I am worthless.")

The placater always talks in an ingratiating way, trying to please, apologizing, never disagreeing, no matter what. He's a "yes man." He talks as though he could do nothing for himself; he must always get someone to approve of him. You will find later that, if you play this role for even five minutes, you will begin to feel nauseous and want to vomit.

A big help in doing a good placating job is to think of yourself as really worth nothing. You are lucky just to be allowed to eat. You owe everybody gratitude, and you really are responsible for everything that goes wrong. You know you could have stopped the rain if you used your brains, but you don't have any. Naturally, you will agree with any criticism made about you.

You are, of course, grateful for the fact that anyone even talks to you, no matter what they say or how they say it. You would not think of asking anything for yourself. After all, who are you to ask? Besides, if you can just be good enough it will come by itself.

Be the most syrupy, martyrish, boot-licking person you can be. Think of yourself as being physically down on one knee, wobbling a bit, putting out one hand in a begging fashion, and be sure to have your head up so your neck will hurt and your eyes will become strained so, in no time at

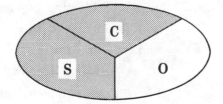

all, you will begin to get a headache.

When you talk in this position, your voice will be whiny and squeaky because you keep your body in such a lowered position that you don't have enough air to keep a rich, full voice. You will be saying "yes" to everything, no matter what you feel or think. The placating stance is the body position that matches the placating response.

(2) **Blamer**

Words — disagree — ("You never do anything right. What is the matter with you?")

Body — blames — ("I am the boss around here.")

Insides — ("I am lonely and unsuccessful.")

The blamer is a fault-finder, a dictator, a boss. He acts superior, and he seems to be saying, "If it weren't for you, everything would be all right." The internal feeling is one of tightness in the muscles and in the organs. Meanwhile, the blood pressure is increasing. The voice is hard, tight, and often shrill and loud.

Good blaming requires you to be as loud and tyrannical as you can. Cut everything and everyone down.

As a blamer, it would be helpful to think of yourself pointing your finger accusingly

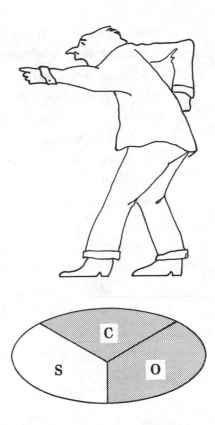

and to start your sentences with, "You never do this, or you always do that, or why do you always, or why do you never . . . ," and so on. Don't bother about an answer. That is unimportant. The blamer is much more interested in throwing his weight around than really finding out about anything.

Whether you know it or not, when you are blaming, you are breathing in little, tight spurts, or holding your breath altogether, because your throat muscles are so tight. Have you ever seen a really first-rate blamer, whose eyes were bulging, neck muscles and nostrils standing out, who was getting red and whose voice sounded like someone shoveling coal? Think of yourself standing with one hand on your hip and the other arm extended with your index finger pointed straight out. Your face is screwed up, your lips curled, your nostrils flared as you yell, call names, and criticize everything under the sun.

(3) **Computer**

Words — ultra-reasonable — ("If one were to observe carefully, one might notice the workworn hands of someone present here.")

Body — computes — ("I'm calm, cool, and collected.")

Insides — ("I feel vulnerable.")

The computer is very correct, very reasonable, with no semblance of any feeling showing. He is calm, cool, and collected. He could be compared to an actual computer or a dictionary. The body feels dry, often cool, and disassociated. The voice is a dry monotone, and the words are likely to be abstract.

When you are a computer, use the longest words possible, even if you aren't sure of their meanings. You will at least sound intelligent. After one paragraph, no one will be listening anyway. To get yourself really in the mood for this role, imagine

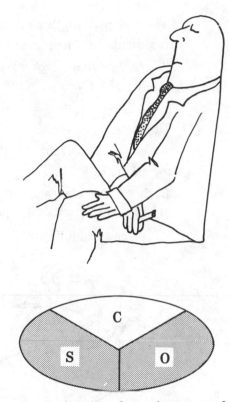

that your spine is a long, heavy steel rod, reaching from your buttocks to the nape of your neck, and you have a ten-inch-wide iron collar around your neck. Keep everything about yourself as motionless as possible, including your mouth. You will have to try hard to keep your hands from moving, but do it.

When you are computing, your voice will naturally go dead because you have no feeling from the cranium down. Your mind is bent on being careful not to move, and you are kept busy choosing the right words. After all, you should never make a mistake.

The sad part of this role is that it seems to represent an ideal goal for many people. "Say the right words; show no feeling; don't react."

(4) **Distracter**

Words — irrelevant — (The words make no sense.)

Body — Angular and off somewhere else.

Insides — ("Nobody cares. There is no place for me.")

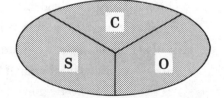

Whatever the distracter does or says is irrelevant to what anyone else is saying or doing. He never makes a response to the point. His internal feeling is one of dizziness. The voice can be singsong, often out of tune with the words, and can go up and down without reason because it is focused nowhere.

When you play the distracting role, it will help you to think of yourself as a kind of lopsided top, constantly spinning, but never knowing where you are going, and not realizing it when you get there. You are too busy moving your mouth, your body, your arms, your legs. Make sure you are never on the point with your words. Ignore everyone's questions; maybe come back with one of your own on a different subject. Take a piece of imaginary lint off someone's garment, untie shoelaces, and so on.

Think of your body as going off in different directions at once. Put your knees together in an exaggerated, knock-kneed fashion. This will bring your buttocks out and make it easy for you to hunch your shoulders and have your arms and hands going in opposite directions.

At first, this role seems like a relief, but after a few minutes of play, the terrible loneliness and purposelessness arise. If you can keep yourself moving fast enough, you won't notice it so much.

As practice for yourself, take the four physical stances I have described, hold them for just sixty seconds and see what happens to you. Since many people are un- accustomed to feeling their body reactions, you may find at first that you are so busy thinking you aren't feeling. Keep at it, and you will begin to have the internal feelings you've experienced so many times before. Then, the moment you are on your own two feet and are freely relaxed and able to move, you find your internal feeling changes.

It is my hunch that these ways of com- municating are learned early in childhood. They represent the best the child can make out of what he sees and hears around him. As the child tries to make his way through the complicated and often-threatening world in which he finds himself, he uses one or another of these means of communicating. After enough use he can no longer distin- guish his response from his feeling of worth or his personality.

Use of any of these four responses forges another ring in an individual's feeling of low self-worth or low pot [see *Peoplemaking*, by Virginia Satir]. Attitudes prevalent in our society also reinforce these ways of com- municating — many of which are learned at our mother's knee.

"Don't impose; it's selfish to ask for things for yourself," reinforces placating.

"Don't let anyone put you down; don't be a coward," helps to reinforce blaming.

"Don't be so serious. Live it up! Who cares?" helps to reinforce distracting.

"Don't let anyone be smarter than you. Be smarter than everyone around you. Explain everything but don't experience it!" [helps to reinforce computing].

[*Peoplemaking*, Virginia Satir, pp. 63-72; Science and Behavior Books, 1972]

Finally, we would add to Satir's excellent description of each of these communication stances the syntactic correlates which we have found to accompany them:

Satir Category 1 — Placater

Use of qualifiers: *if, only, just, even,* etc. Use of subjunctive mood of verbs: *could, would,* etc. Mind Reading violations.

Satir Category 2 — Blamer

Use of universal quantifiers: *all, every, any, each time,* etc. Use of negative questions: *Why don't you? How come you can't?* etc. Cause-Effect violations.

Satir Category 3 — Computer (super-reasonable)

Deletion of experiencer noun arguments — the subject of active verbs as in *I see — can be seen* or the object of verbs wherein the object noun argument is the experiencer, as in *disturbs me — X is disturbing*. Use of nouns without referential indices: *it, one, people*, etc. Use of nominalizations: *frustration, stress, tension*, etc.

Satir Category 4 — Distracter

This category, in our experience, is a rapid alternation of the first three; thus, the syntax which identifies it is a rapid alternation of the syntactic patterns of each of the three listed above. Also, the client displaying this category rarely uses pronouns in his responses which refer to parts of the therapist's sentences and questions.

(*The Structure of Magic, II*, John Grinder and Richard Bandler, p. 53; Science and Behavior Books, 1976)

One way to understand how these postures can be useful in your work is to realize that each of these patterns is useful in coping, given the appropriate context, but that no one of them is complete. Messages about self and context have, for example, been deleted by the placater. Understanding that each of these presents a choice, we, as people-helpers, are able to assist the people with whom we are working to have all of them as alternatives for response. Another way that we have found these Satir categories appropriate to use is that each of the postures represents a universal and frequently occurring pattern of incongruity.

As therapists committed to the profession of people-helping, we are daily faced with the task of responding to non-verbal languages. The problem with which we are faced, then, is how to understand the intricacies and complexities of the unspoken messages effectively enough to assist the person with whom we are working to change and grow. There are two ways which we have found most effective in coping with this difficulty: First, to simply ask what some particular, repetitive body movement, tonality, etc., is or what it *looks* like, or *sounds* like, or *feels* like to him. Secondly, we have found that very dramatic and effective therapy can be based solely on a judgment of match or mismatch, congruent or incongruent, with respect to the messages which we receive.[16]

Notice that neither of these choices requires the therapist to engage in Mind Reading. In the first case, he merely asks for a translation into words (the full Complex-Equivalence relationship), and, in the second case, he assigns no oral meaning to the non-verbal messages he is receiving, but simply decides whether or not the messages fit together. Following are several examples of these patterns, taken from the same transcript further on in the session.

Therapist: Yes, Marcie; and I'm wondering just how you would know when Dave is respecting you.

Marcie: Well, for one thing, he has to learn to pay attention to me; how can he respect me when he doesn't even pay attention to me? Like right now . . .

Therapist: Marcie, how do you know that Dave's not paying attention to you?

Marcie: See for yourself; this whole time, like always . . . I'm talking and he's looking at the floor.

Therapist: So, when you're talking and you see that Dave is not looking at you — then you know that he's not paying attention to you?

Marcie: Good; I see that you've got the picture.

Therapist: Well, I'm not so sure. I'd like you to ask Dave whether or not he was paying attention to you, OK?

Marcie: Yeah, OK. Dave, I would really like to know if you are paying attention to me. (As Marcie says this, she leans forward, with her left index finger extended in Dave's direction, her right hand on her hip, her tone of voice shrill and tight, her throat and neck muscles taut.)

Dave: Of course, Marcie, you know that . . .

Therapist: (interrupting Dave) Hold it a minute, Dave. (turning to Marcie) Marcie, I want to tell about some things I was just aware of when you asked Dave whether or not he was paying attention to you, OK? I had some difficulty understanding exactly what you were communicating. I heard the words which you used, but, somehow, the way that you moved your body, your left hand, and the tone of your voice that you used when you spoke didn't fit for me.

Marcie: Oh, yeah. Well, you're the one who wanted me to ask him. I already knew that he wasn't paying any attention.

Disregarding the patterns which we have already identified, you will notice that the therapist is using his senses — his input channels — to detect incongruity in Marcie's communication to Dave. Specifically, the words which he hears do not match her tone of voice nor her hand movements and positions. Without attempting to assign any meaning to these non-verbal cues, he simply presents them to Marcie and states that he had a difficult time understanding her communication. Consider what has happened here: The therapist detects Mind Reading and Complex Equivalence by Marcie:

not pay attention to me = not look at me when I'm talking

Next, he moves to break up this piece of calibrated communication by asking Marcie to check out her Mind Reading—Complex Equivalence with Dave. As she asks Dave about this, her voice tone, body posture and movements fail to match her words. The therapist again intervenes by making Marcie aware of the incongruities which he detected in her communication and tells her of his difficulty in understanding her incongruent communication. Marcie's response clearly indicates that she is completely calibrated with respect to Dave's communication; she is absolutely convinced that Dave is not *paying attention* to her when he is not *looking* at her. Since she is totally convinced, the task which the therapist has asked her to perform is not congruent with what she believes, and the result is an incongruent communication.

Marcie: Oh, yeah; well, you're the one who wanted me to

ask him; I already know that he wasn't paying any attention.

Therapist: (turning to Dave) Dave, I'd like you to respond to Marcie's question.

Dave: Sure; well, I really was listening to what Marcie (the therapist gestures that Dave should speak directly to Marcie), to what you were saying, Marcie (looking at her). Oh, what's the use (looking down at the floor).

Therapist: Dave, what happened with you just then? You seemed to look at Marcie and then you looked back at the floor.

Dave: Oh, I just saw that look again on Marcie's face. I know what that means: She's unhappy with me.

Therapist: Marcie, true or not true, what Dave said?

Marcie: No. Actually, I was watching Dave's face and thinking how much I'd like to believe him.

Therapist: Dave, tell us about how you end up looking at the floor instead of directly at Marcie.

Dave: What?

Therapist: I'd like you to describe what happened to you when you were talking to Marcie and looking at her, and then you ended up looking at the floor.

Dave: Oh, I'm used to that. I don't talk so good when I get tight — you know, like I was describing before. And when Marcie looks at me that way, I sorta go blank, you know what I mean?

Therapist: And when you are trying to listen to Marcie and understand her, what happens that you end up looking at the floor?

Dave: I really want to hear and understand what she is saying, and if I try to look at her and I see that look

on her face like before, I don't hear what she's saying. Marcie, I really do . . . really.

Therapist: I'm wondering (turning to Marcie) whether
you realized that Dave was not looking at you but
rather at the floor, not because he wasn't paying
attention to you, but because it's really important to
him that he is able to pay attention to what you are
saying. Did you know that before?

Marcie: (beginning to cry softly) Yes, Dave, I believe you.

Therapist: And you, Dave, when you see that look on
Marcie's face — the one that you used to think was
because she was unhappy with you — do you understand that that's Marcie's way of showing interest,
of paying attention to you?

This portion of the transcript shows several important patterns. First, notice that some of the pain connected with Dave and Marcie comes directly from the
calibrated communication system which they have built
up with one another. In the way that Marcie organizes
her experience, she has set up the Complex Equivalence
that if Dave is not looking at her, he is not paying
attention to her. In Dave's way of organizing his experience, whenever he is looking at Marcie and he sees a
certain expression on her face, he has to look away from
her in order to continue to be attentive. This is just the
vicious cycle of communication failure we encounter so
frequently: The very thing that one family member does
to accomplish something is the cue or signal to another
family member that he is *not* doing that very thing. The
cycle continues indefinitely as there is no way in the
present patterns of communication for the individual

members to get feedback.

This exchange between Marcie and Dave, then, is an excellent example of the way in which the patterns of Complex Equivalence and Mind Reading can hook up to create a chain of calibrated communication which results in pain for the family members. We can break up the process in a step-by-step manner to identify the overall pattern and the separate elements of it.

1. Both Marcie and Dave are caring, well-intentioned people. They sincerely want to communicate with each other. Marcie begins to talk; Dave is watching her as he listens.

2. Marcie struggles to express herself accurately, and Dave struggles to understand. In her efforts to communicate, Marcie changes the expression on her face, narrowing her eyes as she makes mental pictures to help her organize her communication (remember, her most used representational system is visual), and leans forward. Dave, in the past, has seen a similar expression on Marcie's face and observed similar body movements by Marcie when she is unhappy with him. That is, Dave has a Complex Equivalence of:

    Marcie narrows eyes and leans forward =
    Marcie is unhappy with Dave

3. By the Complex Equivalence, Dave "knows" what Marcie is feeling and thinking; that is, employing the Complex Equivalence, Dave uses

Mind Reading to determine Marcie's experience. This is the first piece of calibrated communication.

4. Since Dave "knows" that Marcie is unhappy with him, he is tight and finds it difficult to listen and to understand what she is saying while he is aware of her signals. Thus, he shifts his gaze from Marcie to the floor. Notice that this shift comes from his desire to understand Marcie, plus his Mind Reading.

5. Marcie notes the shift of Dave's eyes from her to the floor. In the past, Marcie has seen this movement on Dave's part when he is not paying attention to her. Thus, Marcie has the Complex Equivalence of:

   Dave shifts gaze from Marcie to the floor =
   Dave is not paying attention to Marcie

6. By Complex Equivalence, Marcie "knows" that Dave is not paying attention to her — she "knows" the inner experience which Dave is having. Marcie is now Mind Reading; this is the second piece of calibrated communication.

7. Since Marcie "knows" that Dave is not paying attention to her, she increases her efforts to capture his attention — leaning farther forward in her chair, narrowing her eyes even more, as she attempts to organize her communication more

effectively (by making pictures of the ways she might use to gain his attention). Notice that these changes which she goes through come from her desire to communicate with Dave, plus her Mind Reading.

Dave and Marcie are now locked into a vicious cycle: The more that Marcie tries to express herself effectively, the more she presents Dave with signals that she is unhappy with him, and the more that Dave detects the signal that Marcie is unhappy with him, the more he responds by trying to understand, presenting her with signals that he is not paying attention to her, and the more that Marcie detects Dave's signals, the more she strives to communicate and to capture his attention, and the more .... After some period of time — after the cycle has gone around several times — Marcie will, in fact, become unhappy with Dave, and Dave will, in fact, stop paying attention to Marcie to avoid the bad feeling it gives him. This last step puts the finishing touches on the calibrated communication as it confirms the Complex Equivalence and Mind Reading upon which that communication cycle is based.

In our experience, one of the results of calibrated communication cycles, such as those we have observed between Dave and Marcie, is that, as they continue to miscommunicate in other ways, they come to doubt their worth as human beings. For example, Marcie may come to question whether she is worth Dave's attention, and Dave may come to wonder whether Marcie's being unhappy with him is because he is incapable of being the cause of her experiencing happiness.

A pattern closely connected with one way by which the therapist breaks up a calibrated communication is that of *translation*. Marcie's most used representational system is visual, and, consistent with this, is the type of Complex Equivalence she sets up: Dave is not paying any attention to her unless he is *looking* at her when she speaks. But Dave's primary system for his experience is kinesthetic. Since he *feels* bad (tight and blank) when he sees her look at him in a certain way, he then shifts his gaze to the floor in order to be *able* to pay attention. The therapist recognizes this pattern and states it explicitly, in effect translating from one model of the world (Dave's) to the one which Marcie uses.

Omitting part of the transcript, we come now to another example of incongruity:

Therapist: (turning to the son) OK, Tim, just tell me one thing that you would like to change in your family.

Tim: (glancing quickly at his mother) Well, I don't really know ... Mom always says not to talk about ...

Marcie: (interrupting, leaning forward in her chair, pointing her finger, slowly moving her head from side to side) Go ahead, dear; just say whatever you'd like. (voice tone shrill)

Tim: Ah ... I think that I don't want to ... maybe later.

Therapist: Margaret (15-year-old daughter), when Marcie spoke to Tim just now, what were you aware of?

Margaret: Well, I don't know ... she looked kinda angry and ...

Therapist: What did she say to Tim?

Margaret: Gee, I really don't remember.

There are several useful patterns in this exchange. First, notice that the words which Marcie uses to express herself do not agree with the posture, body movements and voice tonality which she uses as she says the words. The boy Tim (12 years old) must decide to which message he will respond from the conflicting ones he is receiving from Marcie. We can represent this process visually:

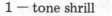

```
                    1 — tone shrill        ⎞
                    2 — finger pointing    ⎬
                    3 — head shaking       ⎠
Marcie                                              ──────► Tim
                    4 — words — go ahead, dear,    ⎞
                        just say whatever          ⎬
                        you'd like                 ⎠
```

Tim decides (not necessarily consciously) to accept the first group of three messages and respond to them rather than to the last single one.

The therapist has identified another piece of incongruent communication — in this case, rather than comment on it himself, he asks another member of the family to do so. Her response allows the therapist to determine several things: Margaret, apparently, is not aware of the incongruity; she reports only the information which she received visually. One of the unfortunate but all-too-common patterns which result from incongruent communication is that the people exposed to it decide to shut down one of their major sources of information. In other words, since the messages which they are receiving do not fit together, their response to this incongruity — the way in which they resolve it — is simply to delete one of the sources of the non-matching messages. In Margaret's case, she is aware of what her mother, Marcie, *looked* like but not of what she *said*.

Several unfortunate things result from this kind of decision on the part of Margaret. First, she has developed a pattern by which, whenever she is presented with an incongruent communication — a situation in which the messages which she is receiving from the other person do not fit — she systematically selects the information which she receives visually. This deprives her of a major source of knowledge about other people and the world around her. Secondly, when Marcie (or anyone) communicates incongruently, she is indicating that she, herself, is uncertain, split, or of more than one frame of mind about what is going on. Incongruent communication is a signal that that person has more than one map or model for his behavior, and that these maps or models conflict. Since these maps or guides for his behavior clash, when he attempts to respond to others, he presents messages from each of these models and the messages do not agree. When Margaret chooses to respond to only one set of messages (derived from Marcie's one model of the world), Margaret loses touch with the other part of Marcie. Each of the models which Marcie has is truly a part of, and a resource for, her. When the people around her come to respond to only one of these parts, Marcie herself begins to lose touch with the other part, and she becomes wholly unaware of this other resource which could be available to her.

Typically, she becomes blocked in her growth and development as an alive and creative human being, her communication remains incongruent, and she feels split, paralyzed — even confused — about what she *really* wants.[17] Thirdly, when Marcie communicates incongruently, other family members are faced with the task of deciding to which set of messages they will respond. Take Margaret as an example: She is only aware of the information she receives visually. Notice that she labels the non-verbal signals: *She looked kinda angry*. This, of course, is a pattern which we have already identified several times, that of Complex Equivalence:

$$
\text{Marcie}
\begin{cases}
1 - \text{tone shrill} \\
2 - \text{finger pointing} \\
3 - \text{head shaking} \\
\\
4 - \text{words} - go \\
\quad ahead, dear, \\
\quad just\ say \\
\quad whatever \\
\quad you'd\ like
\end{cases}
= \ldots kinda\ angry \ldots
\quad \textbf{for Margaret}
$$

This particular Complex Equivalence is likely to become generalized into a piece of calibrated communication — that is, whenever Margaret sees and hears the signals listed above, no matter what else is happening, she will decide (again, probably unconsciously) that Marcie is *kinda angry*. This is the way in which the phenomenon of incongruent communication serves as the basis for establishing the Complex Equivalences from which come Mind Reading and the calibrated communication sequences which are all too often the source of pain. By asking different members of the family to describe their experiences of the ongoing processes, the therapist begins to find out about the rules, the patterns of what the family members *are* allowed, or *are not* allowed, to do, say, or notice about themselves and each other.[18]

One of the classes of rules which is, in our experience, very useful in coming to understand family systems, especially in the context of therapy, is the class of rules about what the family members may perceive and act upon when they experience incongruent communications. Another way of understanding these rules is to determine which input channels the family members may use. These are often the patterns of Complex Equivalence which occur over and over again. The foregoing example of Margaret and Marcie suggests that the information from the *visual* input channel will take priority over the other channels when there is a mismatch.

Another, and in our experience, equally important, set of rules is that which specifies *which output channels* may be used to express *which types of messages* by *which family members.*

Therapist: Yes, Marcie, I understand that you are worried about what Margaret is doing at school. I wonder if you would let her know directly by telling her right now about your concern for her.

Marcie: That's silly; of course she knows that I'm concerned about her.

Therapist: Are you sure, Marcie? How do you *know* that she knows that you're concerned about her?

When was the last time that you told her?

Marcie: Look, things like that don't need to be said; after all, I'm her mother; I mean ... (fading out)

Therapist: Well, just go ahead and try it, Marcie; you know, being her mother and all.

Marcie: Margaret, I ... (pause) ... (Marcie laughs nervously) ... this is really hard. I don't see what ... OK (laugh), I am concerned about you, Margaret. I care about you and what you are doing.

Therapist: (turning to Margaret) Well, Margaret, did you hear what she said?

Margaret: Yeah, I heard ... but it's blowing my mind ... and I like it.

Therapist: Margaret, is there anything that you would like to say to Marcie?

Margaret: Oh, oh ... , mmm, let me see ... well, actually, I do want to tell you that your face looked so nice and soft when you just said what you did. I mean, ... I really liked watching you and hearing what you said, and any time you want to say anything like that again, I'll be glad to listen.

Therapist: Marcie (turning to her), did you hear her? (pointing to Margaret)

Marcie: (crying softly) Yes, I did.

Here, the therapist begins by identifying the by-now-familiar pattern of Mind Reading. He challenges the calibrated feedback by asking the mother to check with her daughter to find out whether or not her hallucination is accurate. Marcie immediately balks. This notifies the therapist at once that a family rule is involved — specifically, the rule that, in this family, the expression of concern by the mother for the daughter (and, in our experience, this rule probably applies to other members of the family as well) cannot be explicitly communicated verbally. In other words, in the terms which we have been developing, the rule eliminates the output channel of verbal expression for messages of concern.

The therapist stays with Marcie, encouraging her until she successfully breaks the family rule against expressing concern through bodily contact. As soon as the mother has accomplished this, he moves to the daughter and works with her to provide positive feedback to Marcie. Then, he extends this new learning, the ability to use the output channel of direct verbal expression to communicate concern, and has the daughter break the rule, also. Next, he creates another option for expressing messages of love and concern within the family system. He guesses at and then verifies that there is a rule against the mother and daughter (and, most probably, the other family members) expressing their love and concern physically — that is, he identifies another output channel which has been knocked out by a rule.

Therapist: I have a hunch about something. Marcie, is there any way that you can imagine that you could, *right now*, express your concern for Margaret?
Marcie: Huh, I don't see how . . . , I . . . no . . . I can't.
Therapist: Well, are you willing to learn another way of expressing your concern for Margaret?
Marcie: Sure, I'm game. I sorta like what I've learned so far.
Therapist: Marcie, I would like you to slowly get up,

cross over to Margaret, and hold her gently.

Marcie: What? That's silly; things like that ... oh, that's what I said the last time. (getting up and crossing the room to Margaret and slowly, at first clumsily, and then more gracefully, embracing her)

Therapist: (quietly turning to Tim) And, Tim, what are you aware of as you watch this?

Tim: (startled) Ahh, I want some, too.

This is an excellent example of the outcome of a therapeutic intervention to assist the family members in congruently expressing their feelings and caring for each other. The therapist assists the members of the family in becoming congruent in the expression of important messages. As this happens, he immediately generalizes this new learning to include other output channels — other choices for harmonious expressions — and other family members.

SUMMARY

In Part I, we have attempted to begin to develop a model of the ways in which we have found it useful to organize our experience in family therapy. We have done this by, first, attempting to find a point of common experience from which to build our model. This point of common experience is a description here in words which each of you can associate with the actual rich and complex experiences you have had in your work as family therapists. As we stated previously, models of experience — our model of family therapy — are to be judged as *useful* or *not useful*, not as true or false, accurate or inaccurate. The first requirement for a model to be useful is that you must be able to connect it with your experience — thus, the need for a common reference point. We have selected language patterns as the common reference point; these constitute the Patterns of Family Therapy, Level I.

The second level of patterns which we have identified involve non-verbal as well as verbal patterns. We have not attempted to be exhaustive — there are many more patterns of which we are aware which we have found to be extremely useful in our work in family therapy. Rather, we have attempted to identify the *minimum* set of patterns which we feel necessary for creative, dynamic and effective family therapy. In the next part, Part II, we will group these patterns into natural classes and specify some of the ways in which we fit them together in effective, larger level patterning. We will also, in this next part, focus more on the choices which the family therapist has in assisting the family members to change the patterns of their system to make possible the process of change and growth, both for each of them as individuals and for the family as a whole.

FOOTNOTES FOR PART I

1. The term *language assumption* or *presupposition* refers to the things which the listener must assume to be true about the world of experience in order for the verbal communication to make any sense at all. For example, if I say to you, either:

(a) *I ignored the ant on my plate.*

or

(b) *I didn't ignore the ant on my plate.*

in order for you to make sense out of what I have said, you must accept a world of experience in which it is true that:

(c) *There was an ant on my plate.*

Each of us as speaker/listener of the language English (the same is true of every other natural language) is constantly using presuppositions in our verbal communications. Learning to understand and use this pattern will increase the effectiveness of your communication. In this volume, we include an appendix, A, which identifies some of the many English forms which carry presuppositions. We also recommend pages 52-53 and pages 92-95 in Volume I of *The Structure of Magic*, Science and Behavior Books, 1975; pages 240-243 in *Patterns of the Hypnotic Techniques of Milton H. Erickson, M.D.*, Volume I, Meta Publications, 1975; and Part II of *The Structure of Magic*, Volume II, Science and Behavior Books, 1976, for a fuller presentation of the various uses of this pattern.

2. The use of the pattern of verbal communication called *embedded question* in the context of hypnosis is presented on pages 237-240 in *Patterns of the Hypnotic Techniques of Milton H. Erickson, M.D.*

3. The use of the pattern of verbal communication called *conversational postulate* or *polite command* in the context of hypnosis is presented on pages 241-246 of *Patterns of the Hypnotic Techniques of Milton H. Erickson, M.D.*

4. The term *referential index* refers to whether a language representation picks out a specific portion of the listener's world of experience. For example, the words and phrases:

. . . this page . . .
. . . the reader . . .

. . . Virginia Satir . . .
. . . the number on this page . . .

all pick out a specific part of the reader's ongoing experience,
while words and phrases such as:

. . . that particular sensation . . .
. . . people who fail to understand this sentence . . .
. . . someone, sometime, somewhere, somehow, something . . .
. . . no one, everybody, all the times I can remember . . .

do not pick out a specific part of the reader's experience. We
recommend pages 47-48 and 80-88 in *The Structure of Magic*,
Volume I; pages 160-177 in *Conjoint Family Therapy*, Science
and Behavior Books, 1964; and pages 217-224 in *Patterns of
the Hypnotic Techniques of Milton H. Erickson, M.D.*, for a
more extended presentation.

5. A fuller presentation of the use of this verbal pattern is available
   on pages 40-43, 49-51, and 59-73 in *The Structure of Magic*,
   Volume I; and pages 209-231 in *Patterns of the Hypnotic Techniques of Milton H. Erickson, M.D.*

6. The process of requesting that the family member specify his
   process descriptions — that is, specify verbs — is one of the ways
   in which the therapist insures that he or she is working with
   the coping pattern in the family member's model of the world
   and not in the therapist's own model projected onto the family
   member. A fuller presentation is available on pages 48-49 and
   90-92 in *The Structure of Magic*, Volume I.

7. The therapist's (or hypnotist's) ability to identify and gracefully
   use the verbal patterns of *nominalization* is one of the most
   powerful verbal intervention patterns of which we are aware. A
   fuller presentation of the uses of this pattern is available on
   pages 43-44 and 74-80 in *The Structure of Magic*, Volume I; and
   pages 162-164 and 229-231 in *Patterns of the Hypnotic Techniques of Milton H. Erickson, M.D.*

8. This category of verbal patterning — Semantic Ill-formedness — is one of the most powerful verbal patterns available to therapists and hypnotists in their communication. See pages 51-53 and 95-107 in *The Structure of Magic*, Volume I; and pages 146-152 and 209-215 in *Patterns of the Hypnotic Techniques of Milton H. Erickson, M.D.* In the references cited, we distinguish three classes of semantic ill-formedness: *Cause-Effect semantic ill-formedness, Mind Reading* and *Lost Performative*.

9. Cause-Effect semantic ill-formedness embodies all of the cases in which one person claims that another person is causing him to experience some feeling or thought, some inner state, without there being any direct physical contact between the two people. Our point is that each of us can come to have a choice about how the words, tones, body postures, movements, etc., of others will affect us. The technique of identifying Cause-Effect semantic ill-formedness by the language form in which it is presented is discussed in detail in *The Structure of Magic*, Volume I, pages 51-52 and 95-98; *Patterns of the Hypnotic Techniques of Milton H. Erickson, M.D.*, Volume I, pages 146-151 and 209-213; and *The Structure of Magic*, Volume II, Parts II, III, and V.

10. Mind-Reading semantic ill-formedness, along with Cause-Effect semantic ill-formedness, is the basis of much of the calibrated communication cycles which result in pain and dissatisfaction for family members. See *The Structure of Magic*, Volume I, pages 104-106, and *Patterns of the Hypnotic Techniques of Milton H. Erickson, M.D.*, Volume I, pages 151-152 and 213-215.

11. *Complex Equivalence* is the relationship between a word or set of words and some experience which those words name. For example, for some people the word *caring* means always responding when help is requested; for others, it means knowing what the other person requires and supplying it without any need for the other to ask; for still others, it means touching gently; looking happy when the other person approaches, etc. Thus, the pattern of Complex Equivalence is roughly the same as the idea of the definition of the word(s) involved; however, Complex Equivalence is *not* of the standard dictionary defini-

tion, but must be relativized to the particular person's model of the world. See *The Structure of Magic*, Volume I, pages 88-90; *Patterns of the Hypnotic Techniques of Milton H. Erickson, M.D.*, Volume II.

12. Modal operators are discussed in more detail in *The Structure of Magic*, Volume I, pages 69-73.

13. *The Structure of Magic*, Volume I, Chapter 1, includes a discussion of these three principles.

14. The notion of representational systems refers to the way in which each of us typically represents to ourselves the world of experience. An extended presentation of this pattern and the ways in which it can be usefully employed is given in *The Structure of Magic*, Volume II, Part I; and in *Patterns of the Hypnotic Techniques of Milton H. Erickson, M.D.*, especially Volume II.

15. This technique — adding representational systems — is metatactic II, discussed in Part I of *The Structure of Magic*, Volume II.

16. Congruency is perhaps the single most important dimension of communication which each of us, as agents of change, can develop — both in being congruent in our own communication and in our ability to detect congruency and incongruency in the communication of others. See Part II, *The Structure of Magic*, Volume II; *Peoplemaking*, Science and Behavior Books, 1972, Chapters 4 and 5; and *Patterns of the Hypnotic Techniques of Milton H. Erickson, M.D.*, Volume II.

17. We recommend that the reader read Parts II and IV of *The Structure of Magic*, Volume II, for an extended discussion of the development and utilization of incongruency in both individual and family therapy.

18. We intend to explore the notion of rules, their development and utilization in therapy, in Volume II of *Changing with Families* (forthcoming). We recommend R. D. Laing's discussion of rules in *Politics of the Family and Other Essays*, Tavistock, London; *Peoplemaking*, Chapter 7; and *The Structure of Magic*, Volume II, Part IV.

PART II

Introduction

In this part of the book, we will present the overall model for family therapy. Models for complex behavior are ways of explicitly organizing your experience for acting effectively in this area. Family therapy is assuredly one of the most complex areas of human behavior. For our model to be useful for each of us as a family therapist, it must reduce the complexity to a level which we, as humans, are able to handle. In the model we present here, we have kept that requirement clearly in mind; we have identified what we consider the minimum distinctions which will allow the therapist to organize his experience in family therapy so that he may act in a way which will be both effective and creative. What this means is that, in our experience, when we are careful to make the distinctions we present in our model, and when we organize our experience in the category specified in the model in the sequence stated, we have been consistently effective and dynamic in our work with families.

In Part I of this book, we identified and gave examples of some of the patterns we consider necessary for effective family therapy. In this portion of the book, we group those patterns into natural classes. These natural classes specify a sequence in which the therapist can, in our experience, usefully employ those first-level patterns — they show him an order in which he may effectively apply the patterns identified in Part I. The result of this grouping is an explicit, formal strategy for family therapy. The strategy is explicit in that it specifies both the parts of the process of family therapy (the patterns of Part I) and the sequence in which they can be applied. Because it is explicit, the strategy is also learnable. The strategy is formal in that it is independent of content — it applies equally well to *any* family therapy session, regardless of the actual "problems" which the family brings to the session. Again, we are stressing that there is a *process* independent of *content*. Our attention is basically on the process. Change the process and new uses of content are possible. The process depends only upon the forms and sequences of the patterns which occur in the communication between the family members and the therapist. For example, the process is independent of the length of the therapeutic session. Another way to explain what we mean when we point out that the strategy given by our model is formal, is to say that the model deals with process — it focuses on the patterns of coping within the family system, irrespective of the specific problems found within that family.

It is important for us to emphasize this distinction between *content* and *process*. Our model of family therapy is designed to assist the family in coping effectively at the process level. In other words, independently of whether the members of the family believe their "problem" to be in the area of sex, or money, or child-rearing practices, in-laws, discipline, or whatever, effective family therapy will expand their choices of expressing congruent communication and of coping in every area of their experience as a family. In our work, we have found that assisting family members in having new choices at the *process* level in *any* area of content will generalize naturally to other areas of their experience.[1]

Furthermore, our model is designed to provide each of you with a way of organizing your experience so that you have a direction, a way of knowing what happens next, not by deciding beforehand what will happen but by recognizing the patterns presented to you by the family. Perhaps most important for your continued growth as a potent family therapist, it provides you with a way of getting feedback, a way of finding out what works. Our hope is that you will accept this model and find it useful in your difficult but rewarding work as a people-helper.

We feel that it is helpful to you, the reader, in using the patterns in the model for family therapy which we have created, to have an explicit, clear understanding of the process we call communication. We would remind the reader that what we present as our model of the word *communication* does not completely cover either our understanding or our experience. Rather, we offer it as a guide to assist you in finding meaning in our model for family therapy. Visually, we can represent the process of communication in the following steps:

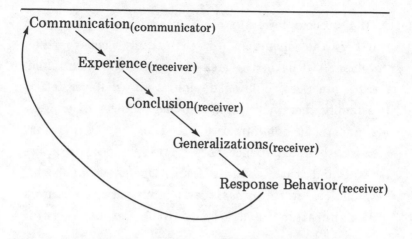

We now present a brief description in words of these specific steps in the process of communication:

(1) Communication (communicator) = the messages offered by the person doing the communicating. The person communicating will present these messages in many different forms — body postures; movement of hands, arms, etc.; eye-scanning patterns; voice tonality and tempo; breathing rate; words, sentence syntax, etc. Furthermore, these messages may or may not be in the conscious awareness of the person communicating.

(2) Experience (receiver) = the messages received by the person to whom the communication is directed. The messages are received through the various sensory channels: eyes, ears, skin, etc. These messages may or may not be in the conscious awareness of the person receiving them.

(3) **Conclusion** (receiver) = the understanding reached by the person receiving the messages as to what the messages mean. Again, the receiver may reach an understanding both in and out of conscious awareness.

(4) **Generalization** (receiver) = the way in which the person receiving the messages connects them with his past experience, and the way in which the receiver uses his understanding of the messages received to shape his comprehensions and responses explain their use in the present and, without intervention, for the future.

(5) **Response Behavior** (receiver) = the way in which the person receiving the messages responds. This step in the communication cycle is equivalent to the first step when the original communicator and receiver have switched positions. In the diagram on page 98, this is the meaning of the arrow which cycles back, connecting the last step in the diagram to the first step.

In our experience, the process of communication between two or more people rarely occurs in this sequence; rather, the steps typically overlap. For example, even as I arrange my body in a certain posture, move my hands and feet and eyes, produce a certain tone of voice, speak at a specific speed, utter the specific words in the specific sentence forms, I see movements as you shift your body posture, move your hands, nod or shake your head, etc. — movements which present messages to me which I incorporate (both in and out of awareness) into my ongoing communication. Thus, as with any model which we create, we have made discrete and separate the ongoing flow of experience in order to attempt to fully understand all of the messages and to create new choices for ourselves.

As family therapists, one way for us to understand the task which we have set for ourselves is to assist the families who come to us in pain to create new choices for themselves, both as individuals and as a family unit. The family's pain becomes for the therapist a signal for a powerful intervention for change. Pain, therefore, is in itself a useful message. We interpret it as a wish to grow in an area in which the person needs help to achieve that growth. More specifically, we work to discover the needs and to help the family members change the patterns of communication by which they are creating this pain for themselves. Using the previously given, five-step model for communication, we ask how we can train ourselves to be more skillfull in discovering the patterns which are causing the family pain, and how we can re-organize the family's resources so as to transform the patterns of pain into patterns of positive communication which each family member can use to gain what he or she wants. Another way of stating this is to ask: What are the characteristics of the patterns of miscommunication in families; by what particular process are they created; and how, specifically, can we intervene in the family system to help the members transform the patterns of miscommunication into resources for themselves? To answer these questions, we will describe two extreme patterns of communication — the pattern of *calibrated* communication, which results in *pain* and *dissatisfaction* for the people involved, and the pattern of *feedback* communication, which results in *choices* for the people involved. Whether the communication is congruent or incongruent, the *process* of communication will continue — in both cases, each of us acts and reacts. Typically, the way we act in the context of *incongruent* communication is untimely, inappropriate, and chaotic, while, in the context of *congruent* communication, we act timely, creatively, and appropriately to the occasion.

CALIBRATED COMMUNICATION CYCLE

We now describe the specific characteristics of a typical calibrated communication cycle[2] which results in pain for the people involved. We use the five-step communication model.

(1) Communication (communicator): In both the formation and the running-off of the calibrated cycle, the person initiating the messages is acting incongruently. In other words, the messages carried by the communicator's body position and movements, his voice tonality, his skin tone and color, the tempo of his speech, the words, the sentence syntax, etc., do not match. Usually, the communicator who is incongruent in his communication is unaware that the messages which he is presenting to the receiver

do not match. This is possible because he is aware of only some of the messages he is presenting — the set of conflicting messages remains outside of his awareness. For example:

George: (head shaking slowly from side to side, breathing shallow and irregular, all body weight on right leg, left leg slightly forward, voice quality harsh and raspy, left hand slightly extended, index finger pointing, right hand extended, palm up) *Ooohh, Mother, how delightful of you to drop in on us.*

Here the messages carried by George's body — his movements, breathing, voice tone and words — do not match. Yet, George, if questioned about it, would very likely be aware only of the words which he uttered and not the conflicting messages carried by his other communication channels. Which set of messages George is most aware of is closely connected to what his most used representational system is. We understand that George, in this situation, is not lying, attempting to deceive himself or his mother-in-law, or even being insincere. Rather, we know that George has several simultaneous responses to unexpectedly finding his mother-in-law standing on his front porch. A part of George responds by attempting to be gracious and welcoming to his mother-in-law; another part of George apparently is startled, upset, and angry, etc. The point for us to make is that each of the messages carried by George is a valid representation of a part of him at that moment in time. To deny, or ignore, or judge as bad any of these messages and the parts of George which produced them is to deny or ignore some important elements of George which can serve as powerful resources for him. In fact, they can serve as an opportunity for growth and change. Furthermore, in our experience, it is, literally, impossible to actually deny or ignore a part of a person; that part will continually assert itself until it is accepted, possibly transformed and integrated into the whole person. One example from traditional psychiatry of this continual assertion of a denied or ignored part is *symptom conversion.* The parts of George which generate the conflicting messages we understand to be inconsistent models of the world which he has not yet integrated.

(2) Experience (receiver): The receiver is now faced with the task of understanding the communication presented by the communicator — a set of messages which do not match, do not fit together. Typically, the receiver will selectively pay attention to the messages arriving through one of his input channels and disregard the others. More accurately, in our experience, the receiver will be aware of the messages arriving in one of his input channels, while the remaining messages are received and accepted outside

of his awareness. Again, which messages the receiver is aware of is closely connected with his most used representational system. The important point here is that, when a receiver is presented with incongruent communication from the communicator, he represents all of the conflicting messages, some within his consciousness, some outside. If the receiver is aware that some of the messages conflict, he, typically, will consciously regard the communicator as insincere or deceitful. If the receiver is aware only of the messages which fit together — the messages which conflict being received and accepted at the unconscious level — then, typically, he will initially become uncomfortable, and, if he continues to receive incongruent communication, after some time he himself will become incongruent in his responses. This description contains the essential elements of the process by which children become incongruent — a natural learning from well-meaning parents. In addition, people who focus on the content rather than the process are vulnerable to incongruity. This process, by the way, is the basis for much of the discomfort experienced by people-helpers who are faced daily with the task of communicating with incongruent people with whom they are working. Some patterns of miscommunication — the processes by which family members create pain for themselves — show up in the systems created between therapists and those with whom they work. This is one of the reasons that therapists themselves frequently feel drained at the end of the day and sometimes have difficulties in their own lives.

(3) **Conclusion** (receiver): Faced with the task of making meaning out of a conflicting set of messages, the receiver, typically, ends up having one of two experiences:

(a) If, in Step (2), **Experience** (receiver), the receiver has organized his reception of the conflicting messages so that he is aware of only the consistent messages, he will reach the conscious conclusion that the communicator intends only the messages of which he is aware. As mentioned previously, he will receive and accept the conflicting messages at the unconscious level, and, typically, will reach the conclusion (at the unconscious level) that the communicator intends the messages received outside of awareness. The outcome of this process is that the receiver creates within himself conflicting models of this experience and usually feels confused.

(b) If, in Step (2), **Experience** (receiver), the receiver has organized his reception of the conflicting messages so that he is aware that they do not match, he will regard the communicator as insincere or manipulative, or even as evil and malicious.

(4) Generalization (receiver): Often, in the context of incongruent communication, previous experiences (especially from the receiver's family of origin) are activated or triggered by the conflicting messages. It may be, for example, that the particular combination of incongruent messages in the specific sensory channels parallels a pattern of incongruent communication from one of the parents of the receiver. Or, it may be that the feelings of confusion experienced by the receiver trigger the recall of experiences from the past in which he also felt confused. If, for example, two people have a history of inter-communication and one of them, when expressing anger, has, in the past, consistently extended her finger, pointing at the second person, then, when she is incongruent in a way which specifically includes pointing her finger, the second person will respond *only* to the pointing-finger portion of the incongruent communication — that is, for the second person:

finger pointing = other person angry

no matter what other messages might accompany the pointing finger. This type of generalization — taking a portion of a complex experience and accepting it as representative of the whole experience — is, again, an example of what we call *Complex Equivalence*. Furthermore, when the second person decides that the meaning of the pointing finger is that the first person is angry, he presents us with a typical example of the pattern which we call *Mind Reading*. One distinctive characteristic of the types of generalization called Complex Equivalence and Mind Reading is their rigidity — their inflexibility. The person making these types of generalizations has no tools for checking to find out whether or not they are accurate. His conclusions are fixed and operate automatically, often independently of the context in which they occurred. We emphasize that generalizations are a tool, an important way of organizing our experience. This book is, in itself, a series of generalizations about our experience in family therapy. It is only when generalizations become fixed and rigid, deeply embedded in the person's perception of inter-communication messages, that he experiences no choice in responding. These generalizations are, literally, presuppositions — a filter of generalizations from his previous experience. They are so deeply embedded in the person's behavior that he will distort the messages he is receiving to fit his generalizations, rather than to come to his senses and directly experience the world. These patterns are powerful examples of self-fulfilling prophecies — they keep the person who operates with them from experiencing the world in the present time and place. They distort fresh experience to fit their previously determined concepts and the world becomes a monotonous rerun of the past. These two patterns — Complex

Equivalence and Mind Reading — form the basis of the calibrated communication cycles which create pain in family systems.

(5) **Response Behavior** (receiver): As mentioned previously, the response can be regarded as the beginning of a new cycle of communication. In addition, unless the receiver of the original incongruent communication is himself congruent, he will respond incongruently and another calibrated communication cycle begins. Therapists need to carefully avoid developing, without their being aware of it, calibrated communication with those with whom they are working in therapy, and themselves reinforcing the destructive patterns rather than developing new choices with the family members. An example of this is the situation in which the therapist responds to an attack by one family member on another member as though he (the therapist) were the one being attacked.

Typically, calibrated communication cycles between members of a family will become more and more abbreviated until merely the raising of an eyebrow will trigger pain and rage in other family members.

We now present an example of a highly calibrated, pain-producing communication cycle from a family therapy session.

The family in this session consists of three members:

Henry — the husband/father: placating, with

a kinesthetic representational system as
primary;

Michele — the wife/mother: blaming, with a
visual representational system as primary;

Carol — the daughter (age 16): super-reasonable,
with an auditory representational system as
primary.

Earlier in the transcript, each of the family members
identified the name of what he/she wanted for himself/
herself (their nominalizations) as follows:

By Complex Equivalence

Henry — Love . . . . To be touched
(especially by Michele)

Michele — Respect . . . . To be looked at

Carol — Equality . . . . To be listened to
(and believed)

Notice in this portion of the transcript the way in which
the experiences each family member wants (their Complex Equivalences) interact so completely that, even
though the original names show little overlap, they fit
together in a tight cycle of calibrated communication.

. . .

Michele: . . . At this point, I don't even care what you do;
I don't see what difference it . . . (left finger pointing,
voice shrill)

Carol: OK (interrupting) . . . I'll just check out then . . .

Michele: ... (interrupting and screaming) Don't you ever turn your back on me, you ...

Carol: But you said that you didn't care what I did so I ... (turning to Henry) ... you heard what she said, didn't you?

Henry: Huh?

Michele: Henry, she's doing it again — she's not respecting me.

Henry: (moving over to Michele's side and placing his arm around her waist supportively) ... Well, perhaps I could ...

Michele: (interrupting Henry) God, Henry, don't paw me — I'm serious about this child's disobedience and lack of respect.

Henry: (voice low and shaky, eyes moist and downcast) I was just trying to ... oh, forget it (turning away).

Michele: Oh, God, not you, too!!

Carol: It's so ridiculous — Mom, I think I'll split, OK?

Michele: ... I couldn't care less what you do now.

Carol: OK, goodbye!!

Michele: (screaming) Young lady, if I've told you once I've told you a thousand times ... Henry, why don't you ever do anything about this?

Carol: But, you said ...

Henry: (overlapping with Carol) Huh?

...

Notice how the seemingly diverse names of what each family member wants (nominalizations) actually interact: Carol wants *equality* — described as an experience, this means that she wants to be *listened to* as seriously as she listens to other family members. Michele wants *respect* — to her, this means that the other family members should *look at* her when she is doing something which involves them. Michele begins by saying (in words) that she doesn't care what Carol does. Carol, with her model of the world (auditory), takes Michele's words seriously and turns away, ignoring the incongruent messages from her mother's body movements and voice tonality. Michele then explodes, as, to her, turning away is equivalent to failing to show respect. Carol seeks support from Henry, asking him to verify what Michele has said. Henry, given his kinesthetic representational system, has missed nuances of the exchange, which required visual and auditory representation for full understanding. When Michele demands that Henry respond to her, he does so in the way which is most appropriate for his model of the world: He moves to Michele's side and touches her. She, however, wants his *visual* attention and fails to recognize the kinesthetic contact by Henry as a caring response. Henry now feels rejected and shows this by turning away, unloved. This, of course, is a signal to Michele that he doesn't "respect" her. Carol now asks Michele for permission to leave. Michele responds to Carol incongruently ... and the cycle begins again. This example shows the way in which very different-sounding words (nominalizations) can be closely connected — so closely, in fact, that they form what we call a calibrated communication cycle.

The remainder of this book presents some of the choices for effective, creative intervention by the therapist in such calibrated communication cycles.

FEEDBACK COMMUNICATION CYCLE

We now briefly describe the way in which the five steps in the communication cycle in which feedback is present are different from calibrated communication cycles.

(1) Communication (communicator): In the case in which the communicator is congruent — all of the messages match — there is no difficulty; the communicator is unified in his expression. In the case in which the communicator is incongruent, he is in contact with his ongoing experience so that he himself will detect the incongruency in his communication. This allows him many choices.

(2) Experience (receiver): If the communicator is congruent in his expression, no difficulty arises. If the communicator is incongruent, the receiver, if aware of the incongruency, has the freedom to gracefully call the communicator's attention to the incongruency, and, if asked, the receiver can then offer additional feedback to the communicator to assist him in integrating the conflicting messages and the models from which they arise. For example, when faced with a person whose head is slowly shaking from side to side, while he states that he really does want to wash the dishes, the receiver may gently comment: "I heard you say you want to do the dishes, and, at the same time, I saw your

head shaking slowly from side to side. I'm wondering if you can help me make sense out of this for myself." The important point here is that the receiver has the freedom to comment and the incongruent communicator has the freedom to accept the comment without feeling attacked, without his self-esteem's[3] being threatened. These are the essential ingredients of communication with feedback.

In the case in which the receiver is initially unaware of the incongruity in the original set of messages, he may only notice a vague uneasiness which marks the discrepancy between the meaning of the messages received at the conscious level of awareness and the meaning of the messages received at the unconscious level. In this case, he has the freedom to mention that he feels uneasy and to explore the source of his uneasiness with the communicator. This requires that the receiver have a sensitivity to his own ongoing experience as well as the ability to explore his feelings of uneasiness without his self-esteem's becoming involved.

(3) Conclusion (receiver): When the messages which the receiver accepts are *congruent*, he has no difficulty in understanding the meaning of what the communicator intends. When the communicator presents *incongruent* messages, whether or not the receiver has organized the conflicting messages so that he is aware that they do not fit, he will reach a conclusion that

something about the communication didn't work for him. This will either occur in the receiver's awareness, and he then will have the freedom to gracefully present the dissenting conclusions he has reached from the conflicting messages and, possibly, even give the communicator specific feedback (for example, that the communicator's body posture did not fit the tone of voice he used) as he explores the specifics of the incongruity with the communicator. If the receiver has *not* been aware of the particular conflicting messages (i.e., when he has organized his experience so that he is only aware of the messages which fit together, the conflicting messages having been received and accepted at the unconscious level), he will, typically, reach the conclusion that he is confused. When the receiver is sensitive to his own experience and recognizes his confusion, he is free to comment on it and has the choice of requesting the assistance of the communicator in resolving it. What is particularly important here is that the receiver and the communicator both have the choice of exploring their communication without their self-esteem's being threatened — without the exchange's becoming a survival issue — using the occasion, instead, as an opportunity for growth and change.

(4) Generalization (receiver): What distinguishes this step in a *feedback* communication cycle from the way generalizations are made by the

receiver in a *calibrated* communication cycle is that, when the incongruent messages are received by the receiver and they trigger some experience from the past, he is sensitive enough to his ongoing experience to immediately become aware that he is only partially present in the interaction — part of his attention has shifted to some other time, place and experience. This allows him the choice of continuing with the communication, refocusing his attention with the understanding that there is something unfinished connected with the particular pattern of incongruency presented by the communicator. He understands that some of his experience at that point in time is coming from somewhere else. He may, of course, comment to the communicator on what is occurring, and he has the freedom to request feedback to help him resolve the unfinished pattern from the past which is presently distracting him.

One way in which the feedback cycle differs from the calibrated cycle is that, whenever the receiver is confused or aware that a previous occurrence is intruding and distracting him from freshly experiencing the present, he immediately attends to that sensory experience to discover what is happening. By being able to immediately establish sensory contact with his present situation and, especially, with the communicator, he can use his experience of confusion or distraction to learn more about himself and the person with whom he is communicating.

This allows him to detect any patterns which are distorting his experience by accepting a part of a message for the entire communication (Complex Equivalence) and patterns of "knowing" the inner experience of the communicator without checking it for accuracy with the communicator (Mind Reading). Thus, the generalizations which the receiver in a feedback cycle makes and uses are flexible guides for understanding which are constantly being up-dated and checked against sensory experience.

(5) **Response Behavior** (receiver): If the communicator began this cycle with an incongruent communication, then either the receiver has detected the conflicting messages in awareness and has begun to explore this with the communicator, using feedback, or he has detected a sense of confusion and has begun to explore this. If neither of these have occurred, then, typically, the receiver's response behavior will reflect the incongruency — that is, the receiver himself will present the original communicator with an incongruent set of messages. If both the original communicator and the original receiver have the freedom to comment on and explore any confusion or incongruity without the interchange's becoming an issue of survival, then, before long, one or the other of the people involved, as they shift from communicator to receiver, will detect miscommunication patterns and begin to explore this opportunity to learn.

One way to clarify the usefulness of these two specific kinds of communication cycles (calibrated and feedback) is to understand that the therapist's task is to assist the family members in changing their patterns of communication from calibrated loops to feedback cycles. (See page 118.) Another way to use this model is for the therapist to check his own communication patterns with the family members to prevent *himself* from being incorporated into their destructive patterns of communication. These specific choices of effective intervention by the therapist are the focus of the remainder of Part II. We offer the five-step communication model for your use in understanding the way in which all of the specific intervention techniques fit together.

We move on now to present in more detail the intervention choices available to therapists, based on this communication model.

The most general level of patterning in our model for family therapy has three phases:

     I. Gathering Information
    II. Transforming the System
   III. Consolidating Changes

I. GATHERING INFORMATION

In the first phase of family therapy, the therapist works with family members to gather information which will help him to create an initial experience with them (Phase II) which can then serve as a model for them in their future growth and change. The question

THERAPIST'S INTERVENTION

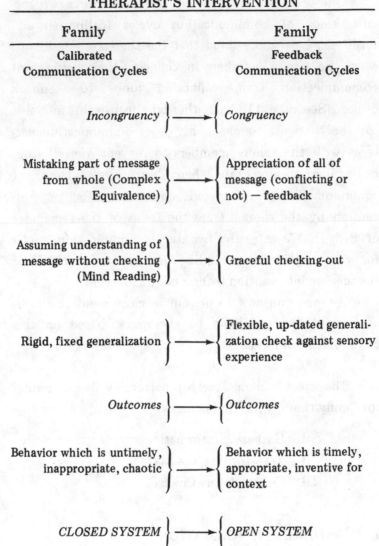

Family	Family
Calibrated Communication Cycles	**Feedback Communication Cycles**

Incongruency } ⟶ { *Congruency*

Mistaking part of message from whole (Complex Equivalence) } ⟶ { Appreciation of all of message (conflicting or not) — feedback

Assuming understanding of message without checking (Mind Reading) } ⟶ { Graceful checking-out

Rigid, fixed generalization } ⟶ { Flexible, up-dated generalization check against sensory experience

Outcomes } ⟶ { *Outcomes*

Behavior which is untimely, inappropriate, chaotic } ⟶ { Behavior which is timely, appropriate, inventive for context

CLOSED SYSTEM } ⟶ { *OPEN SYSTEM*

which the therapist must face is: Which introductory experience will best serve as this model for the family? One of the major purposes of the therapist's actions during this phase is to determine exactly which experience he will, in fact, initially use as a model. We call this set of actions by the therapist *determining the desired state*. Essentially, the desired state is a description of one condition of living for the family which would satisfy the desires of the individual family members. In other words, one of the ways by which the therapist organizes his activities during this phase is to seek out the information which identifies for him the way the family members themselves want the family experience of living to be.

In the process of determining this desired state for the family, the therapist is listening and watching, experiencing the family fully as they begin to make known their hopes and fears about themselves as individuals and about the family as a whole. This identifies the second category of information that the therapist is seeking: information regarding the *present state* of the family. In order to act effectively in Phase II, the therapist needs to know not only what the family wants — which we will call the desired state — but also what resources the family has presently developed.

We emphasize that what we are calling the *present state* and the *desired state* are nominalizations. These nominalizations are useful only to the extent that the therapist and the family members understand that the present state is actually not a state but a *process* — the ongoing interaction and communication. Furthermore, the desired state — the experience which the family members and the therapist will create in Phase II — is actually the first step in the process of opening up the family system to the possibilities of growth and change.

What we have learned in our experience is that the desired state identified by members of the family with the therapist's help, no matter how different are the families themselves, is always a state in which all family members come to behave more congruently than they do in their present situation. Again, for us, congruency is a *process* — the ongoing process of learning and integration.

Which of the patterns of coping which the family and its members present to the therapist can best serve as resources to create an environment for growth and change — whether or not the family members regard these process patterns as resources in the beginning? To create an effective model experience, the therapist needs to understand both the direction of change and the currently available resources of the people with whom he is working.

The third characteristic of creative, effective family therapy occurs during this phase when the therapist is working with the family members to prepare them to *actively participate* in creating the model experience. The act of participating in originating this experience will require that the family members act in ways which are different from the ones they have been using in the past. In other words, they will be taking risks. There are several specific ways in which the therapist can systematically assist the family members in making these revisions. First, the therapist works to build up the family members' trust in him as an agent of change. The ther-

apist acts as a model of congruency by communicating
congruently himself — all of the messages which he presents must match. The way in which he moves must
match the sound of his voice, which matches the words
which he uses, which match . . . . In addition, the therapist must be alert to identify each family member's
most used representational system. When he has determined this, he can increase the confidence of each family
member in him by shifting his own process words (predicates) to the representational system of the person to
whom he is speaking. Even more effective than simply
shifting his process words (predicates) to those of the
family member with whom he is communicating, is for
the highly skilled family therapist to vary the emphasis
which he places on the types of communication systems
which he selects to use with a particular family member.
For example, with a family member whose most used
representational system is visual, the deft therapist
will communicate by using his body, hand and arm
movements — any set of signals which the family member can *see*. With a family member whose primary system is kinesthetic, the therapist will make frequent physical contact, *touching* to communicate or emphasize
certain points he wants to be sure the family member
understands. The therapist uses his skills in communication both to set an example and to make explicit the
process of effective communication. So, for example,
when a family member presents the therapist with a
verbal communication with a deletion which renders it
unintelligible, the therapist requests the missing information rather than hallucinating what it might be. Or,
if a family member is Mind Reading or communicating

incongruently, the therapist may gracefully comment on it — demonstrating both the importance of the freedom to comment and the equal importance of clear communication to other family members. As he communicates, the therapist leaves space for the family members to respond, using polite commands *(conversational postulates)* and embedded questions. He shows that he values the family members' abilities to understand and participate in the ongoing process by inviting them to comment on exchanges between himself and another family member. By these techniques, he makes individual contact with each family member to develop their confidence in the therapist's skill as a communicator and as an agent of change.

The second major way in which the therapist acts to help the family members prepare for change is to share with the family member the information which he has gathered, smoothly using his communication skills to do this. Typically, the family members begin with a statement of what they want for themselves and their family; this statement invariably includes a nominalization. As the therapist gathers information, he is de-nominalizing; that is, he is turning the representation of an *event* into a *process*. One of the things which happen as he does this, and shares the information with the family members, is that the way the family got to the place where they are now is seen as a series of steps of a process. By coming to appreciate their own family history as an understandable, step-by-step process, the family members can have hopes about there being a *next* step in the process which will allow them to make the changes which they desire. The therapist does not, of course, attempt to insure that each family member has the understanding which is his — his task is not to train family therapists. Neither does he keep relevant information from the family. Rather, using his skills as a communicator, the therapist presents to the family members the information each needs to understand that change is possible. As he shares his information about the process of communication in the family, the therapist describes what he experiences — he does not evaluate or make judgments about it. This distinction between the *description of the process* and the *evaluation of other people's behavior* is, in itself, an important learning tool for the family members.

One of the outcomes of the therapist's skillful use of representational systems, congruency and sharing of information with all family members, is that the family members come to understand and trust one another. We find it very rewarding when we are able, through our communication skills, to help one family member come to fully understand that another family member is not being malicious, or evil, or crazy when he does not understand the first member's communication, but, rather, that their communications are simply not making a connection with one another, as each is paying attention to a different part of their shared experience.

Contrary to what many people expect, difference itself can become an opportunity for growth; it contains the seeds of excitement and interest, and the challenge of new learning when guided in that direction. Difference can also, of course, be used negatively; then, sameness can be made a cementing factor. Both sameness and difference are essential, for they manifest the uniqueness of each human being. Much of the therapist's task is to balance these two qualities and, specifically, to use his skills to help the family members to convert the differences which previously caused them pain into an occasion for learning and growth.

When the therapist works with the family to help them to understand the *process* steps by which they got into their present situation, and teaches them the difference between *descriptive* and *judgmental* language, the family often discovers a crippling episode from the past, usually based on miscommunication. This encounter can be used to help them learn that any human experience from the past can be uncovered, understood and utilized.

The result of the processes of developing each family member's trust in the therapist as an agent of change and the therapist's sharing of the information with the family is that the family members become willing to take risks, to venture into unknown territory, and to attempt to build new bridges within the family. By carefully preparing the family members during Phase I, the therapist is able to engage the hopes, energy and creative participation of the family members in developing an experience which will serve as a model for them in their future growth.

Determining the Desired State

The presence of a family in a therapy session is a statement by that family that their present state — their present ways of coping, communicating and interacting — is unsatisfactory to them. It is a statement that the family recognizes, at some level, that there is a discrepancy between what their present experience as a family is and what they want for themselves. The typical case in our experience is the one characterized by the family arriving for the initial therapy session, each member having some idea of what it is that he wants to change. The initial focus of the therapist is to find out what those changes are. The simplest, and a very effective, way of doing this is for the therapist to introduce himself to each of the family members and to ask them what it is, *specifically*, that they want for themselves as individuals and for their family. This process is a model presented to the family to assist them in learning to make meaning congruently. The therapist understands that, while the *content* — the specific hopes of this particular family — is important, the way he secures this information, the powerful *process of communication*, is taking place at the unconscious level, with himself as the model.

> *What do you want for yourself and your family?*
> *In what way, specifically, would you like you*
> *   and your family to change?*
> *What are you hoping for, for yourself and for*
> *   your family, in therapy?*
> *If you could make yourself and your family dif-*
> *   ferent in some way, what would that be?*
> *If I were to give you a magic wand, how would*
> *   you use it?*

Any of these questions will start the process of determining the desired state for the family. As the family members begin to respond to the therapist's questions, they will, typically, present their ideas about what they want for themselves and their family in the form of a nominalization. For example, many families with whom we have worked state that they want more *love, support, comfort, respect*, etc. Each of these words is an *event* representation of a *process*, with most of the pieces of the process missing. The family members, sometimes, will begin by stating what they *don't* want. Using the linguistic patterns presented in Part I, the therapist works with the individual family members to secure positive statements of what they want — statements completely acknowledged by them of what each wants for himself.

As we pointed out in the first part of this book, nominalizations involve the language processes of *deletion, lack of referential indices*, and *unspecified verbs*. For a family member simply to say that he or she wants *more love* leaves out much necessary information — whom does this person want to love or to be loved by, and how, specifically, does this person want the other person (or people) to love him (or her)? By systematically identifying and challenging the deletions, lack of referential indices, unspecified verbs and nominalizations, the therapist gathers the information he needs to understand what the family members want.

During this phase of family therapy, the therapist is making use of his skills as a communicator to connect the words the family members use with what they want. The therapist has connected the family members' words with their experience (has adequately de-nominalized their speech) when his understanding is specific enough that he knows what observable behavior would indicate for that person what he really wants — when he would be able to act out some sequence of behavior with the family member which would be recognized as an example of what that individual desires.

Two general ways of proceeding to adequately connect language and experience (de-nominalization) are:

(a) Employ the linguistic distinctions of deletion, lack of referential indices, unspecified verbs, nominalizations, and modal operators;

or

(b) Have the family members act out a sequence of behavior which is an example of what they want.

These two general ways of starting the process of de-nominalization are, in our experience, more closely connected than the two categories would suggest. More specifically, when a family member is describing verbally what he wants or what stops him from getting what he wants, almost invariably both that person and the other family members will be acting out before your very eyes the thing being described. In other words, family members match their *verbal communication* with their *non-verbal behavior*. Knowing this, the therapist can accelerate the process of understanding what the family member wants by being sensitive to the non-verbal signals which are being sent at these points in the therapy session and then shifting to focus on that process. For us, these two ways of proceeding to connect language with experience are fully integrated. As a guide for ourselves in this area, we invent, both for us and for the family members, experiences which include as many of the sensory channels and representational systems as possible. This action, for us, is a basic assumption about what are the most effective conditions for learning and changing. By choosing to *act out* an experience, rather than simply to *talk about* it with the family, the therapist engages all of the family members' channels for experiences (visual, kinesthetic and auditory).

The process is complete when the therapist understands what kind of observable behavior is an adequate example of what the family member wants — in other words, the de-nominalization is complete when the therapist has established which experience (Complex Equivalence) counts for the family members as an example of what they want.

One of the major tasks for the therapist in Phase I is complete when he has successfully connected language with experience for each member of the family (de-nominalizations). However, there is one very important step remaining for the therapist in this area, as he is attempting to gather information regarding the desired state for the family as a unit. The de-nominalization for each of the family members may result in a set of experiences (Complex Equivalences) which are relatively unrelated. To establish, for the family as a unit, a desired state which will be helpful for the therapist to use to guide his behavior in creating a unified experience with the family, he works to find some way to coordinate the experiences which the family members want for themselves. In other words, he must choose a route to de-nominalization by which the individual experiences (Complex Equivalences) which they want will overlap, or, at least, will connect. Since the therapist is going to use these Complex Equivalences as the basis for creating an experience with the family in Phase II, these experiences to which the family members agree will have to fit together. In the process of delicately and gracefully integrating the different experiences wanted by the separate family members, whatever is common among those experiences will emerge naturally. In our experiences in family therapy, often the most diverse-sounding word descriptions, once connected with experience, will automatically merge for the family members involved.

The therapist can be sure that he has adequately connected the family members' words with experience (de-nominalized the family as a unit) when the result is a set of experiences (Complex Equivalences) which, themselves, connect. As the process continues, if the therapist notices that there is little connection among them, he might ask one of the family members to present (either as a verbal description or in any representational system, e.g., pictures, body movement, etc.) an example of an occasion when he *failed* to obtain the very thing he desired. As one of the family members does this, the therapist might then ask the others how the description or action being presented is connected with what *they* want (their de-nominalizations). In our experience, this has never failed to produce an overlap in the experiences (Complex Equivalences) which the different family members want.

The outcome of the process of making clear what each family member wants is that the therapist and the family both come to understand what the essential ingredients are of an experience which they will co-operatively build as a part of Phase II of the family therapy session. The set of overlapping experiences (Complex

Equivalences) which result from connecting words with experience (de-nominalization) suggest the structure to be used for Phase II. Before the therapist and the family can begin effectively to construct this experience, one other class of information is necessary. Having a map of San Francisco is a valuable asset if you intend to visit and explore that city; however, the map is of little use unless you also know where you presently are in relation to San Francisco. Your map will be useful to you only if you can get to San Francisco from where you are now. The therapist's major task is to assist the family in moving from where they presently are to where they want to be. The other category of information necessary for the therapist is the present resources and current patterns of coping which now exist within the family.

Determining the Present State
(What is Currently Going On)

As the therapist employs the various ways of connecting language with experience and, at the same time, gathers the information necessary to understand the desired state of the family, he is engaged in the on-going process of communicating with, observing and listening to the interaction of the various family members. Thus, while the focus of the *content* of Phase I is the *desired* state for the family, the *process* is the patterns of communication which are available within the family in its *present* state. Every verbal and non-verbal message of each family member and the verbal and non-verbal responses which those communications bring from the other family members constitute the process of coming to understand the family's present state.

The amount of communication which occurs in a family therapy session is enormous — it is, actually, much more than is needed for the therapist to determine the present state of the family system. With this in mind, we have isolated what we consider some of the more informative and distinctive features of family interaction; by isolating them, we are identifying one way for therapists to organize their experience in family therapy so that:

    (a)   They will not be overwhelmed by the complexity of the situation;

and

    (b)   They will detect the processes which will allow them to sufficiently understand the present state of the family system so that they may effectively create, with the family members, the experience in Phase II.

This is simply a way of saying that, in this phase, we are offering a model for family therapy which has been effective and useful in our experience; as with all models, it is neither exhaustive nor unique.

The first of these larger patterns is the calibrated communication cycles which already exist within the family. Typically, the calibrated loops which we encounter are already so established in the family process that the family members regard them as an unalterable part of their experience. Often, the very learning that these cycles can be changed is, perhaps, the most powerful information which we, as therapists, can provide for the family members. Our feeling is that, by understanding the underlying process by which these cycles of pain and miscommunication are created, we, as family therapists, can have more choices about the way in which we assist families both to overcome those loops already present in their system and to avoid forming new ones in the future. The general pattern of the process by which calibrated communication loops are formed in family systems can be represented as:

incongruency → decision → generalization

↳ Conclusion (Complex Equivalence → Mind Reading)

Calibrated Communication

We discuss each of these steps in turn. The process most typically begins when some person in the family communicates incongruently; for example:

Mildred: . . . I just wanted to help you out . . . (voice tone harsh, feet spread apart, standing, left arm extended with index finger pointing, shoulders hunched and tensed, breathing shallow, right hand balled into a fist placed on right hip, . . .

In the example given, the messages carried by the body posture and movements and the voice tonality match with each other but not with the words and syntax of the verbal communication — a classic case of incongruity. When faced with a communication such as this, the person (receiver) typically responds by deciding (step 2 in the process) whether he will respond to the verbal message or the analogue messages.

. . .

George: (reducing his breathing, extending his hands toward Mildred, palms turned up, whining tonality) . . . I'm sorry, Mildred, I don't understand . . .

The other person in this family system decides to respond to the analogue portion of Mildred's incongruent communication. In this case, the decision is to give priority to the analogue messages arriving primarily through the visual channel rather than the auditory (verbal) channel. Now the process of generalization occurs; in this transcript, the person (George) becomes aware that he feels bad, and this is associated (consciously or not) with an entire set of experiences from the past, when Mildred has been angry with him and he has felt bad.

. . .

Therapist: . . . George, what are you aware of right now?
George: Well, my stomach's tight — I feel right bad. (turning to Mildred) Mildred, honey, I know that you are angry and . . .

The next step in the creation of a calibrated communication loop is the Complex Equivalence. The analogue signals or messages which George is attending to are accepted as being equivalent to the inner state labeled "anger" in Mildred. The process is completed with the next step, as George accepts the generalization of the Complex Equivalence itself — that is, anytime in the future that George detects the analogue messages described above from Mildred, he will "know" that she is angry. When this loop has been run often enough, the number of analogue cues which George will need to fire off this Complex Equivalence will be reduced. For example, we have encountered cases of calibrated communication in which the shrug of a shoulder, the change of a breathing pattern, or the shift of weight from one leg to another are messages sufficient to initiate a Complex Equivalence, with the accompanying Mind Reading and a calibrated loop. In each of these cases, the person doing the Mind Reading was wholly unaware of the observable portion of the Complex Equivalence — that is, the cue or signal which "gave" him the information was totally outside of his consciousness.

Another effective way of gathering information sufficient to understand the present state of the family system is to use as leads the nominalizations which the family members claim they want for themselves in the desired state. When a family member identifies the nominalization he wants for himself, he is, in effect, stating that he is not satisfied with what he is presently getting from the family in regard to this nominalization. Thus, as the therapist employs his skills to de-nominalize the family members' nominalizations into some set of Complex Equivalences which will identify actual, observable behavior, he can have the family member give (verbally or by acting out) an example of how what happens in his or her present experiences in the family stops him from getting what he wants. Almost invariably, in our experience, the family member presents a case of calibrated communication which is at the center of much pain and dissatisfaction in the family system.

The two strategies which we have just presented for gathering information necessary to understand the present state of the family system have in common the fact that they identify the patterns of calibrated communication. In our work, we have found that the therapist has information sufficient to understand the present state of the family system when he has identified the major ways in which the family members communicate in a calibrated fashion — the places in the family communication patterns in which there is little or no feedback. The set of calibrated loops in a family system is the set of rules for that system which the therapist needs to know about to understand the way in which the family is failing to cope. Rules or calibrated communication loops are what researchers in cybernetics called *homeostatic mechanisms.* Homeostatic mechanisms are the processes by which a system, whether it is a simple system, such as one for temperature control, or a complex system such as that of a family, maintains itself in the same patterns of functioning and behavior. To change a system, it is necessary to change the homeostatic processes; that is, when the therapist in a family therapy session has identified the calibrated communication loops or rules, he has sufficient information about the present state of the system to effectively begin the process of creating with the family members the experience³ which they have identified as an example of the desired state for them.

Summary

There are three major parts of Phase I of family therapy, Gathering Information. These are:

1. Preparation of family members for creating an experience which will serve as a model for their future behavior;

2. Determining the desired state for the family system;

3. Determining the present state of the family system.

The therapist can effectively accomplish the first of these by working to create confidence and trust in him in the family members and by sharing the information he gathers, especially making sure that each of the family members comes to appreciate the process by which they have come to the situation in which they now find themselves and, thus, allowing them to understand that the change they will make is simply the next step in an ongoing process over which they can learn to exercise control. The main feature of the second part, that of determining the desired state for the family, is the connecting of words with specific experiences (de-nominalization of the nominalizations) which each of the family members brings to the session as his need or hope for himself and his family. The third part is achieved when the therapist has identified the calibrated communication loops which prevent the family from getting what they want for themselves. The therapist and the family members will have a clear direction, once they have determined the present and future states of the family system. This information, plus the family members' preparedness to accept risk, signals to the therapist that the first phase is complete and he may begin to create the explicit experience which will serve as a model for the future of the family system.

The description of Phase I above is an idealized version of our experience, as is any model; it is the minimum effective set of patterns which we have come to distill from our work in family therapy as adequate for Phase I. We have found it extremely useful in organizing our experiences in family therapy. We invite you to try it, change it, modify it in any way which makes it work for you, for your own personal style.

II.   TRANSFORMING THE SYSTEM

Once the therapist has gathered enough information to understand, at least to some degree, the present state of the family system, the state desired by the family, and how the present state, as a system, is closed to the experiences desired by the family members, then he is ready to help create that experience — to take the steps necessary to make it possible for the system to transform itself. When we are training family therapists, the most common complaint we receive is that there is too much to keep track of. The purpose of this book is to assist you in understanding which elements you should pay attention to and which are extraneous. All too often, family therapists expend their major resources in focusing on every detail of the *content* of the problems of family members. The family members, however, are calibrated to the problem — operating on expectations and calibrated loops — and, even though there may be three, four, five or more of them, they have found no solution. Why, then, does the therapist think he can do more? The therapist's advantage lies in the realization that he also has calibrations, and so he focuses, not on the problems and content, but on the *processes* of coping and communicating. This allows him to select useful information from the perspective of process, instead of being overwhelmed by detail. Transforming the system will entail change at the coping level, not at the content level. A change in the *system* of how the people in a family give and receive messages from one another is the goal of family therapy, not the solution of problems — the problems are too many. Every day, people need to learn about coping — they need new tools at the process level. So, the therapist gathers information: a set of hopes (nominalizations) which the family members want, such as more love, affection, privacy, freedom, trust, respect, responsibility, etc. The therapist needs to find out which input channels and which output channels are essential for the family members to know when they are getting what they want. Comparing what is wanted with what is presently possible to express, based on the forms of calibration which exist in the family as they communicate about what it is that they do want, gives the therapist important information. One way to accomplish this is for the therapist to pick one set of hopes (nominalizations) — a desired state — for all family members and then to create, with the family, an experience in this set of hopes (nominalizations) by using all of the techniques which are described here. The result is not just a single experience outside of the system, but, rather, it is something which is more important. In order for the family members to go from their present state to a single experience in the desired state, they must first learn about changing. They will have to break some calibrated loops, open up some new channels; they will find out how all of this can be done by the therapist's becoming a model from which they can learn.

For example, the husband (Fred) wants more attention from his wife (Mary). Mary wants more respect from Fred and their daughter. Daughter Judy wants freedom and the understanding from her parents that she is almost an adult. This constitutes one set of information. When the therapist understands how Fred knows when he isn't getting attention from his wife, Mary — what she would be doing (saying, or acting) that would allow him to know he is getting attention — he has a linguistic de-nominalization of the desired state. The therapist needs this same information for each family member. Next, the therapist will have to discern what it is that prevents each family member from perceiving that he is getting what he wants, or what stops other family members from giving him what he wants. This is a second important set of information. For example, Fred might say, "I know my wife is paying attention to me when she is being affectionate and she is *touching* me." This means that all of the attention Mary gives Fred which is not kinesthetic (touching) is outside of Fred's experience. Presently, he can detect and appreciate attention only through his skin and not through his eyes. So, when Mary is paying attention to Fred but not *touching* him, he doesn't respond. The result is that Mary feels that Fred doesn't respect her.

These sets of information can be compared to help you understand this process of coping which is not coping at all with respect to the desires of the family members.

The desired state is outside of the limits of a system which is closed in this way. The task of the therapist is to lead the family members to the experience of getting what they want with three general strategies:

(a) Intervention by challenging fixed generalizations from the past (calibrated communication cycles);

(b) Giving perspective of process (achieving meta-position to system processes);

(c) Transforming the system by re-calibration.

These three tactics will overlap with respect to individual techniques, but the result will be to teach the family the skills of all three strategies, as well as helping them obtain what they desire. So, transforming a system is really adding to the system the tools necessary to achieve any desired state, by showing the family members how it can be done. The family will learn tools to break calibrated communication, tools to focus on process, and tools to communicate in new and more satisfying ways. This is what makes the task of a family therapist primarily that of an educator.

Tools for Intervening to Challenge Fixed Generalizations from the Past (Calibrated Communication Cycles)

In order for a therapist to help create an experience which is an example of the desired state but which is outside of the possibilities of the present state of the family system, calibrated loops will have to be broken. Family members will have to *see, hear,* and *feel* in new ways so that they can *respond* in these new ways. The transformations which are necessary for this to take place must start with the therapist. He will have to intervene in the ongoing process and provide new examples of how to respond and how to understand those new responses. Interventions which break calibrated loops can occur at any of the five transition points from which they were originally constructed:

1. Person *A* communicates incongruently;

2. Person **B** decides to which message he will respond;

3. Person **B** generalizes about his feelings and his decision about the messages;

4. Person **B** builds fixed generalizations (Complex Equivalences);

5. Person **B** Mind Reads Person *A* (is calibrated).

The therapist can intervene at one or more of these points. A complete intervention will require that the therapist break in cyclically through this process until the calibration is broken and the family members learn how to get *feedback* instead of calibrated communication. The particular content of the broken calibration is important only with respect to achieving the goal of providing an experience which is an example of the desired state. The real value of the intervention is the degree to which it teaches the family members that feedback will get them more of what they want than will calibrated communication and that they will learn much more about the other family members when they use feedback to break calibrated loops on their own.

Breaking Calibrated Communication Loops at the Transition Point of Incongruity

Fred tells his wife, Mary: "I want you to be more loving with me." His tone of voice is harsh and demanding, his eyebrows are raised, and his head bobs up and down as he finishes with a sigh, as though he is scolding a child for the hundredth time about not doing his chores. Mary tightens up and moves back slightly in her chair. (The therapist recognizes this pattern from earlier discussions.) Mary, if the therapist permits it, will repeat her part of the calibration loops. She will respond to Fred's tone of voice and his body gestures by Mind Reading *specifically* that he is trying to "put her in her place." At this point, the therapist chooses to intervene at the transition point of Fred's incongruity. Since both Fred and Mary are calibrated in this content area, the task will be to break that calibrated loop for both of them. This has two steps: First, to teach Fred that the way he looks and sounds does not match his *intent* and his words — that his outsides do not match his insides — and to try to teach Fred to communicate both sets of messages congruently, one at a time, instead of incongruently, both at once. This teaches Fred a new way to communicate, and, at the same time, presents Mary with communication which doesn't have two conflicting messages from which she must choose.

Therapist: I heard you say in words that you wanted Mary to be more loving. I also heard a tone of voice and saw you move and gesture in a way which didn't look like you were loving when you said it to her. (The therapist demonstrates Fred's communication, exaggerating the analogue tones and gestures.) Could you put in words what you were feeling when you did this?

Fred: (sighing, as he recognizes the analogue communication) Yeah, well, it is like I've been through this before, and, well, I ask and she just pulls away from me anyway.

Therapist: So you're feeling kind of helpless, but at the same time you do want more loving actions from Mary?

Fred: Yeah, I guess I do feel kind of helpless (sounding and looking helpless).

The therapist at this point can make it even more of a learning experience for the family by presenting Fred with two examples of the same communication. For example:

Therapist: Fred, I understand now that you do feel sort of helpless when you try to communicate your desire for connection with Mary, and I would like to help you. When you ask for contact with Mary, for her to be more loving, you said she seems to just pull away more. Is that right?

Fred: Yes.

Therapist: Well, Fred, I am going to be you and you be Mary. I am going to ask you for contact for loving twice, once like I experienced *you* doing it, and

once in another way. Would you just sit and watch
and listen, and see if you can understand Mary's pulling away?

Fred: Sure.

The therapist then presents Fred with two models or examples of communication, one incongruent, the other
congruent with matching tones, gestures and words. Then,
the therapist asks Fred to try it in this new way. When he
does this, Mary's response is to take his hand.

The point is that people are not aware of their incongruity, and intervention at this transition point provides an opportunity for learnings which can permeate any
areas, independent of the specific content. The person who
learns of his incongruity, as well as those who watch and
listen to this process, discovers that there is more going on
than he ever realized. This leads us to the second transition point at which a therapist can intervene to break
calibrated loops.

Breaking Calibrated Communication Loops at the
Transition Point of Decision

When Fred initially made his first incongruent communication, Mary responded by tightening up — she was
calibrated (operating on a fixed generalization from the
past) to respond only to his analogue communication.
As she observed the process of the therapist's teaching
Fred about the difference between his *intended* message
and the *outside result*, she was also learning about how
she was calibrated to ignore other messages from Fred.
She did not acknowledge his words, only his tone of
voice and his gestures. In essence, she decided that the

analogue message was the *real* message and responded only to it. The therapist could have chosen to intervene at this transition point first; for example:

Therapist: Mary, as I heard Fred ask for you to be more loving, I saw you flinch, and I'm wondering what you saw, heard, and felt as he said this.

Mary: Oh, he was just criticizing me again. I never am sensual enough for him.

Therapist: I heard him ask for something for himself. I wonder if you could say what made you feel as though he were criticizing you. Was it his tone of voice or the way he looked? Did you not believe what he was asking?

Mary: It was like he was yelling at me for making a mistake. Hummmm ... I guess I don't believe he was *asking* but that he was *telling* me.

Therapist: Would you like to check that out? I have a guess at this point in time that Fred has some trouble asking directly for things for himself, that maybe he believes he won't get it anyway, so he asks in a very clumsy way. I think that maybe you don't know how to understand any better than he knows how to ask. I think that there is something here for both of you to learn, if you would be willing. I would like to check it out with him and try to find some way through this block.

From this point, the therapist can teach Mary that both sets of messages she receives are valid, and that she has been responding only to one of them — to a gesture and tone which she doesn't understand. By asking, she can get

helpful feedback; by continuing with the calibrated communication, she will only feel bad. At the same time, this
teaches Fred that his message was clumsy, and that Mary's
response was to his *non-verbal* message. Furthermore, his
understanding of her response was a misinterpretation of
her non-verbal message.

Breaking Calibrated Communication Loops at the Transition Point of Generalization

The therapist may also choose to break the calibration at the transition point of *generalization*. When Mary
heard Fred's incongruent communication, she made a decision to pay attention only to the non-verbal part of that
communication. Just as Fred didn't understand that his
output did not match his intent, so, too, Mary did not
understand that her response did not match Fred's intent.
His gestures and his tone of voice were not congruent for
Mary with *asking* — they were congruent with her experience of *demanding*. She had the feeling that he was criticizing her, telling her that she felt a certain way, the way
she feels when she is being criticized, and was demanding something, so she generalized.

Let's examine the process of generalization more
closely.

> (1) Fred is incongruent in his communication,
> presenting Mary with sets of messages which do
> not match. Specifically, he consciously intends
> to ask her for more loving, and his words match
> his conscious intent; he also feels helpless, and
> this feeling (largely outside of awareness) is

reflected in his tonality, body posture and gestures. . . .

(2) Mary must now respond. She sees Fred's body posture and gestures and hears his tone of voice, and she responds to that set of messages rather than to his words.

(3) In her past experience with Fred (and others), the tonality she presently hears and the body posture and gestures are associated with demands he has made on her.

(4) Mary's decision in step (2) above, plus her past experience with the part of Fred's incongruent communication to which she is attending and responding, lead her to the generalization that Fred is demanding something from her.

(5) In the past, these demands, for Mary, have been connected with feelings of helplessness and anger at the unfairness of being imposed upon. Her response to Fred, then, is based more on these past feelings of anger and helplessness than on the present time-place situation.

The therapist needs to be aware that surface communication often contains deeper messages which, if uncovered, can help to establish feedback. This process of generalization constitutes another transition point at which calibration can be broken. For example:

Therapist: Mary, as Fred just asked you a question, I was wondering what this was like for you. How did you feel as Fred just asked for you to be loving?

Mary: Well, I felt like he was scolding me, telling me what I should do.

Therapist: Could you say what made you feel that way?

Mary: Well, he looked disgusted and he sounded angry.

Therapist: How did you feel as he did this?

Mary: I guess I felt defensive, pushed.

Therapist: Mary, when you see Fred looking disgusted and sounding mad, as you described he just did, does that mean he is criticizing you and pushing you?

Mary: Of course; he does that kind of thing a lot.

Therapist: Oh, so that's it. Mary, have you ever had the experience of being disgusted with yourself, or mad at yourself, and so when you spoke to someone else, it didn't come off quite the way you meant?

Mary: Well, yes; but this is different — he does this a lot.

Therapist: You're so very sure? Is it possible that this big, strong guy over here maybe doesn't feel that strong on the inside, so, when he talks to you about something which is important to him, it doesn't come out quite right? Is that a possibility?

Mary: Well, I guess so.

Therapist: Would you like to find out? I have a hunch that when Fred feels low and looks and sounds like he just did, you take one look at him and go, "Oh, my God; what have I done now?"

Breaking calibrated communication at the transition point of generalization requires that the therapist have access to some experience which the family member has had which contradicts the generalization. Or the therapist can simply *create* one by checking out the generalization with the other family members. Generalization can also be broken linguistically by *exaggeration.* For example, the therapist could say:

Therapist: Mary, if you believe this, both you and Fred are in a real bind. Do you mean that Fred has to wear a perpetual smile and always sound happy or you're being criticized and demands put upon you? That sounds like a terrible burden for both of you. Is that what you're telling me?

Breaking Calibrated Communication Loops at the Transition Point of Fixed Generalizations from the Past (Complex Equivalence)

Fixed generalizations from the past is the next transition point in calibration loops and is also another juncture at which the therapist can intervene. Mary can be helped to build a program which, for the most part, will be outside of awareness, and which has the following steps:

When Mary thinks that someone is angry at her, she feels bad in a certain way. At some other point in time, when Fred is communicating with her, but he is not angry at her, if she feels bad in that same way, then she has a fixed generalization which says, "If I feel bad in this specific way, then Fred must be angry at me."

Mary has come to experience her world in a certain way, and she has learned to move in that world by paying attention exclusively to certain clues from outside of herself, while, at the same time, ignoring all of the other messages she is receiving. This limits what is possible for her to experience. By making it possible for Mary to accept and act on the other, presently unnoticed, clues, the therapist helps her to break the fixed generalization that has held her in bondage. In other words, when Fred is angry and demanding, he presents a whole set of messages. When he communicates incongruently, he presents a *small part* of the messages which he uses when he is angry. Mary is calibrated by fixed generalization to interpret *any* of the analogue communications which occur when Fred is angry to mean that he *is* angry. So, by her calibration, she responds to only a part of Fred's total message. One choice the therapist has here is to make the Complex Equivalence explicit — to label it — and then to demonstrate that it is not necessary and, in fact, distorts the communication process.

Mary: Yes, I know what he was saying: That I'm not good enough and he is tired of it and that I don't give enough.

Therapist: That isn't what I heard. What makes you think he means you're not good enough and that he is tired of it?

Mary: Well, look at him.

Therapist: What is it about the way he looks that makes you think he is tired of you and that you're not being good enough?

Mary: He *always* looks that way when he is tired of my making the same mistake, even when it is just not balancing my check book.

Therapist: So, if Fred makes that particular face, then

anything he says means he is tired of your making some mistake?

Mary: Yeah; well, it sounds kinda . . .

Therapist: What if he makes that face and tells you he has to go to the bathroom, is that your fault, too?

Mary: Well, no.

Therapist: Then it's *not* always?

Mary: No.

Therapist: Is it possible that Fred could mean something else and maybe you're just using that face as a way to be hard on yourself? Is that a possibility, maybe? (She nods "yes.") Let's find out, shall we?

Here the therapist has a chance to give new meaning and, therefore, new choices for responding to familiar behavior.

Breaking calibration loops in this way not only teaches that, just as family members are not mediums who can read minds, neither are they such good logicians, either. Most importantly, the therapist provides a model for family members to use when they have been — or suspect they have been — misunderstood. They learn that feedback works two ways, that uncovering the process beneath a response can be a tool to understanding as well as to being understood. The success of the therapist in breaking calibrated loops will be the model for family members later on, and the experience will also be an incentive for further change, especially when it is done lightly, gracefully, and without blame.

Once one of the calibrations is firmly enough established in the patterns of interaction of a family, the responses may be so programmed that, if one member does X, then another member automatically responds with Y.

For example, the dialogue which occurs when one family member begins to speak and another member says, "I know what you're thinking; you don't have to tell me," is typical of what we term Mind Reading. At this point, the therapist has the choice of cutting into the Mind Reading just long enough to break the calibration. This simply may require repetitiously interrupting the pattern until the interruption itself becomes part of the process, so that intervention toward breaking the calibration can occur. For example, every time Amy begins to speak, her husband, Bill, starts to shake his head back and forth "no" before she has uttered more than half a word. Amy immediately flies into a rage, which is just what Bill claims he knew was going to happen. At this point, Amy tries to reply, stating that it is making her mad, but, as she begins to speak, Bill again starts to shake his head. In order to change this pattern, the therapist needs to interrupt long enough to gain the attention of the family members. For the therapist to make the same criticism as Amy offers would only serve to set up the same system for Bill *with the therapist* as he has with Amy. Here is where humor and pattern-interruption become powerful tools. The therapist tells both of them to stop.

Therapist: You said earlier, Bill, that you would like to get some peace and quiet and that you would like Amy to stop nagging you. Is that true?

Bill: That's what I said.

Therapist: I believe I can help you get it if you will try a little experiment with me. Are you willing?

Bill: Shoot.

Therapist: I would like you to place your hands on your

head, one on each ear, and to do this tightly. If Amy begins to yell or nag, then clamp your hands down tight so you can't hear her. And, while you're doing this, you might use your hands to hold your head still, because I've noticed that, just as Amy begins to speak, your head rocks back and forth, and both of you get dizzy and start hallucinating. Do you know what I'm saying?

Bill: (chuckling, and Amy chuckling, too) All right, all right.

Therapist: Now, Amy, this is your big chance to say what you want to Bill, but remember, if you yell or nag, he will clamp his hands down. So, don't get dizzy, OK?

Amy: (laughing) He looks cute that way.

Therapist: I'm wondering if maybe he doesn't look like this most of the time to you?

Amy: Yes, I believe he does, but when I see it like this, I have to laugh instead of getting angry.

Therapist: OK. Now maybe we can begin to build some channels for you to *really hear* each other, but you will have to go slowly and not get dizzy for a change. Are you both willing?

This kind of pattern interruption (non-verbal exaggeration with humor) provides a vehicle to slow down the process long enough to get something new through the calibration loops. At the same time, another dimension can be added to the process, one which also affects the decision transition point by adding to the picture the message which was deleted by the calibration. For instance, in this particular case, the therapist might add these instructions to Bill:

Therapist: Now, Bill, as you hold your hands over your
ears so you can protect yourself if Amy yells, I want
you to repeat over and over, out loud, "Don't say
anything bad or loud, I'm too fragile." And, Amy, as
he does this, I want you to yell as loud as you need
to in order to get Bill to hear you: "I'm not yelling;
just listen to me, I'm not yelling." OK, now both of
you do this *at the same time.*

The result of this kind of intervention is commonly that
both family members have an experience which is familiar
and, at the same time, humorous, with no blame, neither
of them being the culprit. At the same time, they will get
tired of the silliness and then will be ready to try a new
way, after being presented with an exaggeration of the
complete cycle all at once. The techniques for breaking
calibrated Mind Reading are as numerous as the creativity
of the therapist. The process, however, is always basically
the same: To identify Mind Reading and make the process
by which it occurred obvious enough to both parties
that the need for feedback itself becomes apparent. We
often end up saying to family members, "Do you have a
license for fortune telling? Are you sure you have the
credentials; I didn't know they were giving them out!"
Then two things can be learned by the family members:
First, how to break through calibration loops without
blame, and, second, how to establish feedback. Breaking
calibration loops opens the door for family members to
begin to appreciate the different ways each family member gives and receives messages. The most important learning here is that what is *intended* is not always what is *received.* Or, as we like to say, *the map is not the territory.*

When two people have different maps, they may not be of the same territory. If they then compare the differences without blame, the experience will provide a better guide for both travelers. Arguing about which map is the true map is a sure-fire sign that both individuals have forgotten that *neither* is.

Giving Perspective of Process
(Achieving Meta Position with Respect to System Process)

The three general strategies which we are presenting in this section will, to some extent, overlap; the difference will be more of the focus of teaching. They are provided as guides to organize your behavior, not distinctions in the territory which are isolated from one another. With this in mind, we turn, now, to the concept of assisting family members to gain perspective of system process. For a therapist to help family members to achieve this, he needs to put it in a concrete form so that the family members can understand it, and that they are given a chance to see, hear, and get their gut feelings involved. System process is the ways that all of the patterns which we are explaining in this book fit together. The therapist will be able to open up a family system only to the degree that he can represent to himself that the *problem* is not the problem — the *patterns of coping* are the source of the individual problems. So, when a family comes in and a wife says that her husband, Tom, is unreasonable because he refuses to let her go out and get a job and have a career of her own, and Tom loudly rebuts with: "Your responsibility is to the children at home, and there is no way that I will stand for your robbing them of having a mother and a secure childhood with contact and love" —

then the therapist's task is *not* to say who is right or who is wrong; it is not his domain to arrange a compromise. The resolution of the problem is not the main task of the therapist. Even if this problem is resolved, the calibrated communication which caused this problem will just produce another one. The task of the therapist, then, is to break the calibrated communication loops and to provide an environment for learnings about what choices and resources the family have which they can use to solve *any* specific problems. The therapist's jurisdiction is *process, not content*, the process of how each family member can achieve the hopes which the problem-solving represents (as an example). His task is to add to that process so the family members can resolve their own problems without further assistance. Then, each new conflict is an opportunity for every member to get what he wants. So, system process is the level of patterns to which the therapist is sensitive. He wants to understand *what* and *how, not why*. He strives to assist all members of the family in establishing feedback. If the family therapist does not operate at this level, he will get entangled and become part of the process, which will result in further difficulty.

For example: If the therapist were to ask Tom why he objected to Amy's going to work, Tom would probably elaborate on what he has already told the therapist and, in so doing, increase the demand on the therapist to judge who is right and who is wrong. Instead, if the therapist asks Tom *how* he is succeeding in his aim to give security to his children, and *how* Amy is in agreement with this aim, then the therapist's questions will yield information and awareness which will enable the pair to make a start in a new direction. Asking Tom *why* he does not

want Amy to go to work only reinforces the old tend-
encies. The therapist, himself, needs to develop perspective
at the process level. What this means is that the therapist
must become freely involved, with his eyes, ears, and body
responding to the family members, while, at the same time,
remaining outside of their family system. The therapist is
involved in the *process* of exploring, feeling his way, taking
steps and risks. The family members are involved in
content, trying to get their way, to look good, not to be at
fault. They are trying to find a way to cope with today —
the therapist is educating them with tools which will be
resources for them for the rest of their lives. To provide
learnings which will permeate a family system in this way,
the therapist needs to add another dimension to the transformation of the family system. This is accomplished by
simply providing the family members with a new perspective, a view from *his* eyes of their own system. Breaking
the calibration will succeed only to the extent that family
members learn that they must get feedback and break
calibrated communication loops. Family therapy becomes
even more pervasive when the therapist adds to this his
own explicit perception of system process, from inside as
well as from outside. Family members, involved in *content*
with each other, at a point in time need to stop and tune
in to *process*, to get a perspective which will enable them to
go further. Staying with content has limited possibilities.
Many content issues can be resolved with the new ways of
coping, once the family members begin to understand their
system and obtain the tools necessary to make it work
for them. Our goal is to get as many of these tools in the
hands of each family member as is possible. Our approach
is that problems are endless. The therapist is in a no-win

situation if he uses a "problem-centered" approach. There-fore, we use a "new-coping" approach. The problem is not the problem; *coping* is.

One of the most powerful techniques to achieve per-spective of process of which we are aware at this time is *sculpturing*, by which the therapist translates the family's processes into body postures and movements which repre-sent the communication he has observed in the session. For example:

A father, Jack, might start out standing erect, with a rigid body, his head tilted up, appearing super-reasonable, a pillar of strength which is impenetrable. As he does this, his wife, Joyce, is kneeling in front of him in a wor-shiping, admiring position, staring up. Meanwhile, one by one each of their three children climbs onto Jack's back, until he can no longer bear the weight and collapses to the floor. At this point, Joyce springs up, taking a blaming posture, pointing her finger, her nostrils flaring, until Jack finally struggles to his feet and becomes a stiff board again so Joyce can kneel and worship him.

This visual display presents family members with a picture of process. It allows them to see how the patterns of their communication cycle change the content while the process remains the same.

Added perspective can be achieved by the therapist's describing the process as he moves the family members through this physical, as well as visual, process:

Step One: Jack stands erect, Joyce kneeling, children be-ginning to climb on Jack.

Therapist: I see Joyce appearing to admire Jack's ability to hold things together, being so smart and being someone she can look up to, while the kids are pulling on him to get some attention because he is always so busy keeping things together, and you people want some connection with this big, strong, smart man. And he is tough to get through to, so you pull harder and climb on him more to get him to notice you. Maybe you get in trouble in school so he has to help you with your homework. Or, you could ask him a continuous stream of "why" questions, and, because he is so smart, he'll have to answer. Meanwhile, you, Joyce, look on, admiring his ability to hold things together, until Jack, who looks so sturdy, suddenly falls down and has another breakdown. Now you kids can have contact — he can spend time with you, but poor Joyce is abruptly thrown into the position of keeping everything together. And where is her big, strong man? He now needs her to take care of *him*, so she nags him and nags him and finally reproaches him into getting back on his feet. Finally, Jack gets so scared of what Joyce might do that he struggles up and pretends that he is as strong as an ox. Now, he has to leave behind him his connection with his children, because he has to work extra hard to make up for the time he was sick. You kids miss him, so you begin to climb on him once again.

This adds yet another dimension to the process picture. The therapist can go even further and ask family members to report on their internal experience as they move through this process ballet. Jack, for instance, who is standing strong and erect, might say he actually feels lonely and like a tree branch which is about to break. While Joyce is blaming a broken Jack, she might report that she isn't really mad but scared and desperate. This, too, can add perspective to process. It might be carried yet another step by asking each family member, in each position, what would take off the strain. Jack might ask Joyce to stand up and help him instead of admiring him. As she stands, she might say, "I always wanted to help you and be on the same level with you, but I thought you could only stay strong if you thought I was weak and *needed* you to be that way." This kind of perspective on process not only removes blame and breaks calibration, but it also gives the family members an awareness of the process. This provides yet another choice for the family members to focus on in times of trouble. Before, they only had one perspective, their own. Now they can add to that a perspective of process and an awareness of how each family member's perspective of the same process can be different.

A perspective of system process provides family members with a tool to use to share their different perspectives without fault-finding. This offers family members the opportunity to learn about the various choices available to them within their own family system to send and receive messages. They have a tool to comprehend these differences and to learn from them. Of course, not every family will achieve this perspective in one session; each family will develop a sense of process at its own speed, an inch at a time, and each inch will be valuable to them. The overall strategy of the therapist in assisting families to achieve this perspective requires that he is comfortable with being patient, and that he is able to tap the family's own sources of inventiveness to find ways of allowing them to achieve this perspective of process.

We wish to emphasize that the particular examples which we have presented here are precisely that — examples. Our hope is that each of you will use your ability to create interesting and dynamic variations on these examples. However, we would make two suggestions:

(1) Fully use the skills and resources of the family members. For example, if a family member is a sculptor or painter, or a musician, encourage them to use those mediums for learning.

(2) Involve the maximum number of channels for learning when creating an experience — all of the input channels (the senses), all of the representational systems, and all of the output channels. Using this principle will encourage maximum learning by all of the family members.

The crises which occur in families present all of the members with situations in which they struggle to maintain a sense of self-worth. They are caught in a vortex. It is up to you, the therapist, to distill from the data the process description in clusters of information, and to present it in a non-judgmental way, so that, instead of having to understand innumerable bits of content, the family members need only to cope with three or four steps of process. They then can gain a perspective from which to start to grow.

Transforming the System by Re-calibration

Although the most well-formed outcome of family therapy is a completely open system, with perspective, feedback, freedom to explore and take new steps, this is not achieved by the therapist's attacking and breaking calibration loops at random like a bull in a china shop. A family system is a delicate structure which serves as the basis for interaction of a group of human beings who are not perfect and who don't need to be. Who can become enlightened overnight? Patience is a prime tool for the successful family therapist. It is not our job to thoroughly transform an individual family member. This could well result in that member's becoming alien to the system, thereby placing even more stress on it. The family therapist's task, rather, is to transform the system *as a whole* to a point wherein stress and strain are reduced, and nurturing and support can develop, so that all family members can continue to grow. Family therapists should not be trying to gain every possible inch from every family member, but, rather, they should be feeling their way, looking for a minimum amount of change for maximum results, while, at the same time, teaching family members how to use feedback instead of calibration and how to achieve perspective of system process.

Concentrating on achieving the maximum amount of change with a particular family member can result in skewing the system. Each family already has the possibility of change; our task is to increase those possibilities, those choices for growth and change for *all* family members. One of the most delightful experiences we can have and one which we continually work to create is that which we call the *snowball effect* — a therapeutic intervention which results in the family members' taking charge of the process of change themselves. Too rapid a change will dis- rupt the family system; too slow a change will discourage the members of the family who desperately want some new choices and experiences for themselves. This is the trickiest part of family therapy, to evolve the system as a whole to a point at which it provides a solid foundation of support among family members who have the tools with which to proceed in a certain direction. This is the state wherein individual family members feel free to make choices for themselves. The therapist should re- alize that family therapy is based upon the understanding that every change in any member of a family system has a ripple effect on every other family member. So, if little Johnny, say, is catatonic, to focus our energies on curing Johnny's symptoms will be futile, since, as soon as he returns to the family system, he will respond to that sys- tem in the same old ways, unless the *patterns* of that system have been changed.

Actually, focusing on the family member who has the symptoms is taking the hard path. In order for Johnny to overcome his catatonia directly, he will have to change a tremendous amount and in many ways, especially if the change is to survive when he returns to the original family system. However, if each member of the system changes only a small amount, in a few ways, then the result is that the changes will permeate the system, and Johnny's symp- toms will become unnecessary. Checking this principle is easy if you review your own experience. If you have left home and gone to college or gone in the service, or even moved away and then returned to visit your original family or old friends, you can remember how all of you had evolved and changed. So, at first, it was an awkward situation for you, and, in some cases, it may have remained that way. You returned alien to the former system, and this is just what we must avoid in family therapy if the result is to be an environment in which every member can be nurtured and can grow from the foundation of support for each which the family system will provide.

Imagine that you are standing in front of a stack of glasses, water glasses, which have been carefully placed in a pyramid so that each row of glasses supports the row above it. The top row has one glass, the next row has four glasses, the next row has nine glasses, and the one underneath that row has sixteen glasses. Each row of glasses provides a structure to support all of the glasses above it. If you wanted to take these same glasses and build a new structure which would give you greater choices about how you approached the task of getting a glass, you would not start by pulling glasses from the bottom row; you would not even take all the ones on the left. You would have to start at the top, working down a row at a time, or you would have only destruction. This is somewhat similar to how a therapist should proceed through a family therapy session. Viewing the family through the metaphor of the pyramid of glasses will help to remind the therapist that he should not succumb to the temptation to remove the glass with the smudge on it without any reference to the possible effect of his action on the other glasses.

To organize this process, you can make a rule that every interaction which opens a door or breaks a calibration must be understood by all the family members who observed it. It goes something like this:

The therapist has an interchange with the husband/ father and breaks a calibrated loop which the father has about his son's communication. The therapist then turns to the son to make sure that the boy has also broken his part of the calibrated loop and understands that the father has changed (re-calibrated). The next step is for the therapist to address himself to the mother, who has been observing, and to assist her in understanding and accepting the change in the relationship between her husband and her son. This cycle goes on, each step leading to the next, and all members tuning in as changes occur. This process also accompanies moves to achieve perspective with respect to family process, rotating from person to person, breaking calibrated loops and then re-calibrating the rest of the system to this new part. The whole process of transformation then becomes, in a sense, a new chain in which each link now connects with the next one. This guides the therapist in establishing the best speed and direction for that particular family's system. It provides a safeguard against random jumps which might unbalance the system. Thus, breaking calibration, achieving perspective with respect to family process, and constant forging of new links in the family system are the structure and strategies which weave together the individual interventions to transformation of a family system. These constitute the second phase of a family therapy session, and they also build the road which leads to the third and final stage of a family endeavor. In a sense, we, as therapists, work to reclaim the banished parts, to awaken the sleeping parts, and to connect these newly available assets for greater energy and strength. Thus, we are not really *adding* anything to the family system; we are only making

available to the family members for new uses the resources
which were already there.

III. CONSOLIDATING CHANGES

In the third and final phase of the family therapy
session, the therapist works to consolidate the changes
which the family members created as part of the model
experience in Phase II. We have identified three parts to
this phase:

(1) Review of process of the family therapy session;

(2) Getting feedback regarding the process from
each member;

(3) Developing and assigning homework.

This final phase is an important step in each session,
whether or not the specific experience which the family
members and the therapist identified in Phase I actually
happened in full detail in Phase II. The fact that the family
members and the therapist have been engaged in the
process of working cooperatively to create something for
themselves, is the foundation of every session. Again, the
process is the foundation for change, not the specific
content. Seen from this perspective, each interview session
has a life of its own; it has a wholeness of its own. Contin-
uity is established by developing new building blocks at
each meeting of the therapist with the family.

The purpose of the therapist's actions in this, the

final phase of the session, is to assist the family members in solidifying the gains which they secured for themselves in the session, in effect building a new family history, which now becomes a base for new confidence in taking risks to change and grow. Verily, family therapy occurs in the real world, with real time constraints. But, when a family therapy session is over, the family members have the opportunity to try their new wings on their own. The therapist works to create the conditions which will make it possible for the family to continue the process of change between sessions — the returning family will be different from the departing one.

Review of the Process of the Session

A family has just involved themselves in a therapeutic session whose announced purpose is to assist the family in change. As we emphasized in our presentation of Phases I and II, the key to effective intervention by the family therapist is identifying and breaking calibrated loops in the communication patterns existing among the family members — that is, supplying explicit, conscious feedback in the patterns of family communication where it no longer exists. This review has, essentially, the same elements of process, the process by which the therapist, again acting as a model of congruent communication, provides specific feedback about the session to the family members. This review of the therapeutic session by the therapist is consistent with the principle of assisting the family members in coming to understand the process by which they arrived at the place where they are now. The therapist begins his review by reminding the family members of the state which they were in when they first came to this therapy session, and then, step by step, he recounts the processes which have occurred: What happened during Phase I, the ways in which they all worked together to understand what they wanted, and then prepared to create a new experience in growth for themselves; what happened in Phase II, actions specific to the therapist and to each of the family members.

This review gives the therapist the opportunity to teach the family members his understanding of his experience in working together with them for change. He identifies the steps which he considers important in the process of family change, e.g., the identification of calibrated communication loops. He states how, in his perception of the process, the family members worked cooperatively to create new choices for themselves. He carefully enumerates the steps taken by the family in the process of gaining these new options. By this description of the process of the therapeutic session, the therapist makes explicit the tools and skills which the family needs to continue the process of growth and change which they have begun. In our experience, the most desirable outcome of a family therapy session is not simply achieving an experience which the family can use for future growth, but also is *understanding* that experience, and learning the specific tools which the therapist and the family members employed in the process of its creation. More desirable than just creating an experience of what they want is the explicit learning of the skills necessary to give them new ways of communicating as a family. When this last kind of learning occurs, they move to a truly open system, one which allows them to cope creatively and effectively with any disturbances which might arise, regardless of content, a system which has, and can continue, to use effectively the patterns of coping which they, themselves, have established. The outcome which delights us the most is a family therapy session which ends with the members understanding the process which occurred in it (thereby determining the direction for continued change by identifying the next step) and explicitly learning the tools/skills/steps in the process. Such a session affords us the opportunity provided by the experience of entering a room with closed windows, opening the windows and discovering yet another room with closed windows but also with the keys (tools) needed to enter the next one and the next one.

Getting Feedback from Family Members

Consistent with the principles of acting as a model for effective, clear communication, is the therapist's recognition that the process of feedback in an open system flows in both directions; thus, he insures that each and every family member has the opportunity to comment on his experience of the process of the therapeutic session. At the same time, of course, this checking-out with each family member allows the therapist and the other family members to comprehend the changes they have begun, to understand the way in which they can make meaning out of the process which they have been experiencing in the session, and to appreciate how they have learned the tools of the process of change. During this time, in addition to commenting on the session, the individual family members have the opportunity to ask questions to clarify portions of their experience which they do not fully understand, thus making available to them the tools which they need for further growth, and, thereby, breaking the last of their old rules. This activity also provides the therapist with a chance to help them to make sense out of their experience of the process of change in which they have involved themselves, and, further, allows him to change and to understand the new choices now available for *himself*. If we finish a session and have failed to learn something from it, we take it as a message that, somehow, we were out of tune with this family.

Homework

The process of change and growth for the family which begins in the therapeutic session does not stop when the session comes to an end. As the family returns to their home, the experiences which they created with the therapist in the family therapy session serve as a model for further change. One of the things which the therapist strives to accomplish in his review is to present the process of change which was begun in the session in such a way that the next step in the ongoing process is apparent; thus, the family will be conscious of *how* they may choose to continue their growth after the session.

We have distinguished three kinds of homework assignments which we have found useful in our family therapy work. The first assignment is for the family to set aside a *specific* time and place in their home wherein they can practice what we call *interrupt signals*. When the family leaves the therapeutic session, no matter how effective, dramatic and far-reaching are the changes which they succeeded in making, they return to an environment which is associated in their experience with the patterns of calibrated communication which they are changing.

The physical surroundings, alone, are a powerful stimulus for the re-activation of the cycles which have caused them so much pain and dissatisfaction in the past. In addition to the tangible environment, the experiences associated with work and school, and the everyday activities of daily life today, conspire to activate the old destructive patterns. Interrupt signals are cues upon which the family members agree (usually selected by them just prior to ending a therapeutic session) and which any member of the family may use whenever he detects one of the patterns of calibrated communication which they have been working to change. The therapist should be alert to assist the family members in selecting appropriate signals. These cues are chosen by considering:

(a)   The calibration pattern to be interrupted;

(b)   The capabilities of the family members involved.

For example, if the pattern to be interrupted is one in which a family member *refuses to listen* to the other members of the family, then an interrupt signal which is *auditory* will *fail* to be effective, while a kinesthetic and/or visual signal would be appropriate. An example of the way the therapist should consider the capabilities of the individual family members is the one which we use in families with children. We have found it more effective to plan interrupt signals which do *not* depend upon verbal skills. In our experience, the use of *sculpturing postures* as an interrupt signal for families with youngsters has been very effective. We have found that this cue, once properly selected, must be practiced by the

family. By setting aside a specific time and place for practice in interrupting the destructive patterns, the family
members are more likely to be able to use them effectively
under stress, when they are actually needed. The practice
sessions for interrupt signals can provide an occasion for
fun and laughter for the family when approached as a form
of entertainment or as a game.

The second class of homework is scheduled times
and places for the family members to practice the *specific*
forms of *feedback* which they have developed in the
therapeutic session to replace the calibrated communication loops which they succeeded in changing. During these
sessions, the family members create, by acting out experiences which were formerly connected with the calibration
loops, by fantasy role-playing (fantasizing, and then presenting situations in which the family members can
imagine the former calibration loops' being activated), or
by any other means which they are able to develop so
that they can give each other feedback. We suggest to
families that, during these exercises, one of the family
members not involve himself directly in the feedback
exercise, but, at its conclusion, offer feedback to the
other members who were directly interacting and providing simultaneous feedback. This outside member also has
the agreed-upon authority to stop the exercise if he decides that the feedback is being changed once again into a
form of calibrated communication.

The third kind of homework which we have found
useful is scheduled sessions in which the family explicitly
review the tools/skills/steps in the process of change in
which they are all involved. This kind of exercise is different
from the second kind in that the family members are not

practicing specific kinds of feedback in specific kinds of situations, but, rather, they are identifying and using the techniques of change at the level of *coping*. For example, the family might discuss and role-play the way in which they, along with the therapist, discovered and broke a calibrated communication loop in their last therapeutic session. Then, the family members apply the specific process steps which they have identified in that experience to their ongoing interaction since the last therapeutic session, attempting to become aware of, and break, additional calibrated loops. Again, in this type of exercise, we suggest that one of the family members remain outside of direct involvement in the process for control over the whole. This kind of exercise is designed explicitly to continue the process of change, and to give the family members the skills they need to open up their present system. We call this the process of becoming *congruent* — the process in which people who formerly felt *compelled* now feel free to *choose*. Risk-taking becomes the order of the day; the opportunity to try new things is shared, when love, caring, excitement — all become a part of what we believe is the ultimate meaning of living.

SUMMARY

We have stated time and again, in as many ways as were appropriate for this book, that the overall task of the family therapist is to assist the family members in transforming compulsive patterns of behavior into patterns of *choice* — choices of open, creative behavior. We have presented many patterns which we hope each of you, as

STEP 1 — The Therapist Being the Connector

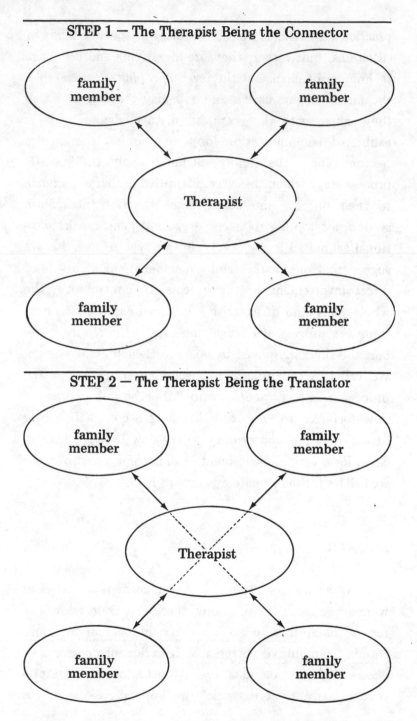

STEP 2 — The Therapist Being the Translator

STEP 3 — The Therapist with the Family on Their Own

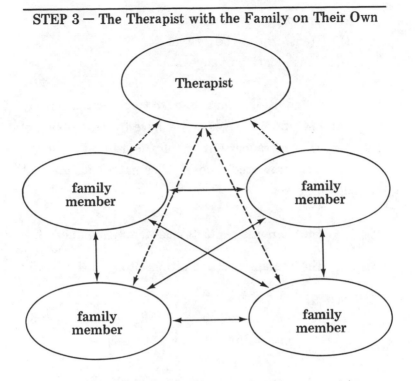

family therapists, will find useful in your work. In this first volume, we have limited ourselves to the minimum patterns which we felt are necessary for effective, dynamic family therapy. The more advanced patterns — including the meta patterns — we hope to make the subject of Volume II. One of the meta patterns — the structure of the way in which the patterns themselves can be organized — is the way that the patterns we have presented in this volume may be sequenced for effective therapy. The basic structure of Part II of this volume is one such meta pattern, the natural grouping of the patterns of Part I under the headings of:

  I. Gathering Information
  II. Transforming the System
  III. Consolidating Changes

We offer one additional meta pattern (represented visually on pages 174 and 175) which we have found to be very effective. This meta pattern is fully consistent with the meta pattern presented above. This meta pattern has the following steps:

1. The therapist contacts each family member;

2. The therapist acts as a translator for the family members;

3. The therapist assists the family members in making contact directly among themselves.

We invite the reader to sort for himself into the three stages of this meta pattern those patterns identified in Part I.

FOOTNOTES FOR PART II

1. This phenomenon, in which changes occur in areas of behavior not expressly dealt with in the therapeutic session, is discussed in *The Magic of Patterns/The Patterns of Magic* (forthcoming, Bandler and Grinder). The key concept is that of isomorphism, same-form pattern. Thus, if an individual makes a change in the area of the way he relates to his *mother* — that is, he gains new choices about how he relates to his mother — then, typically, he surprises himself with a change in his behavior about the way he relates to his *wife, the women with whom he works* at the office, etc. The specific principles by which such

changes are generalized will be presented in the reference cited above.

2. Calibrated communication, as with all of the processes of communication, is not an inherently bad or pain-producing process. It is the basis for close teamwork, whether in the context of co-therapy, ballet, team sporting events, etc. However, just as with each communication and modeling principle of which we are aware, such calibrated communication processes must be checked for their usefulness. When these processes lead to pain and dissatisfaction for the family, they must be re-examined and new choices must be developed. Gregory Bateson presents an excellent discussion of the differences between feedback and calibration in his article, "The Biosocial Integration of Behavior in the Schizophrenic Family," in *Therapy, Communication and Change*, D. D. Jackson (ed.), Volume II; Science and Behavior Books, 1968, pp. 9-15.

3. By self-esteem we mean the person's understanding of his own worth as a human being. See *Peoplemaking*, Science and Behavior Books, 1972, Chapter 3, and *Conjoint Family Therapy*, Science and Behavior Books, 1972, Chapters II and VI, for an extended discussion of this concept.

4. The reader who has had some experience with hypnosis will recognize this principle as being the same as that known in hypnotic work as *utilization*. See either Erickson's discussion directly in *Advanced Techniques of Hypnosis and Therapy*, Grune and Stratton, 1967, J. Haley (ed.), or *Patterns of the Hypnotic Techniques of Milton H. Erickson, M.D.*, Meta Publications, 1975, Volumes I and II.

Epilogue

In this book, we have emphasized the factors of change and the process for how to use them, as we understand them. We want to make it very clear that this process would be an inhuman endeavor without human caring and empathy, and without an eye to the soul and person of the individual in front of you as well as yourself. Refining the ability to find and discriminately use the parts of the change process which we have described will greatly enhance your understanding, and will help you to engage more economically in a productive, therapeutic adventure. Without the humanity, it becomes just plain brainwashing.

Further Reading

When we finish a book, we are oftentimes in the mood for exploring a little further and maybe reaching into some adjoining areas.

If that is now true for you, here are some other books and films to explore.

Barbach, Lonnie G., *For Yourself: The Fulfillment of Female Sexuality*. New York: Doubleday & Co., Inc., 1976.

Bernhard, Yetta. *How to Be Somebody*, Open the Door to Personal Growth. Millbrae, Calif.: Celestial Arts, 1975 (paperback).

Bernhard, Yetta. *Self-Care*. Millbrae, Calif.: Celestial Arts, 1975.

Birdwhistell, Ray L. *Kinesics and Context*, Essays on Body Motion Communication. New York: Ballantine Books, Inc., 1970.

Brooks, Charles V. W. *Sensory Awareness.* New York: The Viking Press, 1975.

Drakeford, John W. *Do You Hear Me, Honey?* New York: Harper & Row, 1976.

Huxley, Laura. *You Are Not the Target.* New York: Fawcett World Library, 1965 (paperback).

Luthman, Shirley, with Martin Kirschenbaum. *The Dynamic Family.* Palo Alto, Calif.: Science and Behavior Books, Inc., 1975. Also available in Swedish, Dutch, Danish and German.

Lyon, Harold C., Jr. *It's Me and I'm Here.* New York: Delacorte Press, 1974.

Miller, Sherod (ed.). *Marriages and Families, Enrichment through Communication.* Beverly Hills, Calif.: Sage Publications, 1975.

Missildine, W. Hugh. *Your Inner Child of the Past.* New York: Simon & Schuster, Inc.

Nierenberg, Gerald I., and Henry H. Calero. *Meta-Talk,* The Guide to Hidden Meanings in Conversations. New York: Cornerstone Library Publications, Reprint, 1975 (paperback).

Phelps, Stanlee, and Nancy Austin. *Assertive Woman.* San Luis Obispo, Calif.: Impact, 1975 (paperback).

Rogers, Carl R. *Becoming Partners,* Marriage and Its Alternatives. Center for Studies of the Person, La Jolla, Calif.: A Delta book, 1972 (paperback).

Satir, Virginia. *Conjoint Family Therapy,* rev. ed. Palo Alto, Calif.: Science and Behavior Books, Inc., 1967 (paperback). Also available in Japanese, Dutch, French, Italian, Swedish, German, Danish, Norwegian, Spanish and Portuguese.

Satir, Virginia. *Peoplemaking.* Palo Alto, Calif.: Science

and Behavior Books, Inc., 1972 (paperback). Also available in Dutch, Danish, Swedish, Hebrew, German and Spanish.

Satir, Virginia. *Self Esteem*. Millbrae, Calif.: Celestial Arts, 1975 (paperback).

Selye, Hans. *Stress of Life*, rev. ed. New York: McGraw-Hill Book Co., 1975.

Selye, Hans. *Stress Without Distress*. New York: New American Library, 1975.

Simeons, Albert T. *Man's Presumptuous Brain: An Evolutionary Interpretation of Psychosomatic Diseases*. New York: E. P. Dutton & Co., Inc., 1961 (paperback).

Smith, Gerald W. with Alice I. Phillips. *Couple Therapy*. New York: Macmillan Publishing Co., Inc. (Collier Books), 1973 (paperback). Original title: *Me and You and Us*. New York: Peter H. Wyden, Inc., 1971.

Smith, Gerald W., with Alice I. Phillips. *Couple Therapy*. Dictionary. New York: Peter H. Wyden, Inc., 1975.

Spitzer, Robert S. (ed.). *Tidings of Comfort and Joy*, An Anthology of Change. Palo Alto, Calif.: Science and Behavior Books, Inc., 1975.

Thommen, George. *Is This Your Day?* New York: Avon Books, 1976 (paperback).

Tiffany, Donald; Julius Cohen; Keith Ogburn; and Analee Robinson (eds.). *Helping Families to Change*. Hays, Kansas: The High Plains Comprehensive Community Health Center, 1972.

Posters by Virginia Satir:

"Goals for Pairing" and "Declaration of Self Esteem." Celestial Arts, 231 Adrian Road, Millbrae, CA 94030.

Videotapes by Virginia Satir:

Family Therapy I: Family in Crises; Communication I: Lectures and Demonstrations; Communication II: Mini-Lecture and Experiential Examples. Science and Behavior Books, Inc., P.O. Box 11457, Palo Alto, CA 94306.

Films with Virginia Satir as consultant:

Insights (22 minutes); *A Better Place to Stand* (25 minutes). Manitou Programs, Inc., I.D.S. Center — 49th Floor, Minneapolis, MN 55402.

Bibliography

Ashby, W. R. *An Introduction to Cybernetics*. Chapman and Hall, Ltd., and University Paperbacks, 1956.

Bach, E. *Syntactic Theory*. New York: Holt, Rinehart and Winston, Inc., 1974.

Bandler, R., and Grinder, J. *Patterns of the Hypnotic Techniques of Milton H. Erickson, M.D.*, Volume I. Cupertino, Calif.: Meta Publications, 1975.

Bandler, R., and Grinder, J. *The Magic of Patterns/The Patterns of Magic*. Cupertino, Calif.: Meta Publications, forthcoming.

Bandler, R., and Grinder, J. *The Structure of Magic*, Volume I. Palo Alto, Calif.: Science and Behavior Books, Inc., 1975.

Bateson, G. *Steps to an Ecology of Mind*. New York: Ballantine Books, 1972.

Bever, T. G. "The Cognitive Basis of Linguistic Structure." In J. Hayes (ed.), *Cognition and the Developments of Language*. New York: John Wiley and Sons, 1970.

Castaneda, Carlos. *Journey to Ixtlan*. New York: Simon and Schuster, 1972.

Castaneda, Carlos. *Tales of Power*. New York: Simon and Schuster, 1974.

Dimond, S., and Beaumont, K. *Hemispheric Functions in the Human Brain*. New York: John Wiley and Sons, 1974.

Gardner, H. *The Shattered Mind.* New York: Alfred Knopf, Inc., 1975.

Gazzaniga, M. *The Bisected Brain.* New York: Appleton, Century and Croft, 1974.

Grinder, J.; Bandler, R.; and Cameron, L. *Neuro-Linguistic Programming,* Volume I. Cupertino, Calif.: Meta Publications, Inc., 1976.

Grinder, J.; De Lozier, J.; and Bandler, R. *Patterns of the Hypnotic Techniques of Milton H. Erickson, M.D.,* Volume II. Cupertino, Calif.: Meta Publications, 1976.

Grinder, J., and Bandler, R. *The Structure of Magic,* Volume II. Palo Alto, Calif.: Science and Behavior Books, Inc., 1976.

Grinder, J., and Elgin, S. *A Guide to Transformational Grammar.* New York: Holt, Rinehart and Winston, 1973.

Haley, Jay (ed.). *Advanced Techniques of Hypnosis and Therapy: Selected Papers of Milton H. Erickson, M.D.* New York: Grune and Stratton, 1967.

Haley, Jay. *Strategies of Psychotherapy.* New York: Grune and Stratton, 1963.

Haley, Jay. *Uncommon Therapy.* New York: Grune and Stratton, 1968.

Kartunnen, L. "Remarks on Presuppositions." At the Texas Conference on Performances, Conversational Implicature and Presuppositions, mimeograph, March 1973. Kartunnen has a series of incisive papers on presuppositional phenomena in English. We suggest you write to him directly at the University of Texas for copies.

Kuhn, Thomas. *The Structure of Scientific Revolutions.* Chicago: University of Chicago Press, 1962.

Jackson, D. D. (ed.). *Communication, Family and Marriage.* Palo Alto, Calif.: Science and Behavior Books, Inc., 1968.

Jackson, D. D. *Therapy, Communication and Change.* Palo Alto, Calif.: In J. Hayes (ed.), *Cognition and the Developments of Language.* New York: John Wiley and Sons, 1970.

Laing, R. D. *The Politics of the Family and Other Essays.* London: Vintage Books, 1972.

Miller, G. A.; Galanter, E.; and Pribram, K. *Plans and the Structure of Behavior.* New York: Holt, Rinehart and Winston, Inc., 1960.

Montagu, Ashley. *Touching.* New York: Harper and Row, 1971.

Perls, F. *The Gestalt Approach: Eyewitness to Therapy.* Palo Alto, Calif.: Science and Behavior Books, Inc., 1973.

Polster, I. and M. *Gestalt Therapy Integrated.* New York: Bruner/Mazel, 1973.

Poloya, G. *Patterns of Plausible Inference.* Princeton, N.J.: Princeton University Press, 1954.

Pribram, Karl. *Languages of the Brain.* Englewood Cliffs, N.J.: Prentice Hall, 1971.

Sapir, E. *The Selected Writing of Edward Sapir.* D. Mandelbaum (ed.). Berkeley: University of California Press, 1963.

Satir, Virginia. *Conjoint Family Therapy.* Palo Alto, Calif.: Science and Behavior Books, Inc., 1964.

Satir, Virginia. *Peoplemaking.* Palo Alto, Calif.: Science and Behavior Books, Inc., 1972.

Watzlawick, P.; Beavin, J.; and Jackson, D. *Pragmatics of Human Communication.* New York: W. W. Norton and Company, 1967.

Watzlawick, P.; Weakland, J.; and Fisch, R. *Change.* New York: W. W. Norton and Company, 1974.

Whorf, B. "Grammatical Categories." In J. E. Carroll (ed.), *Language, Thought and Reality.* New York: John Wiley and Sons, 1956.

Appendix A

SYNTACTIC ENVIRONMENTS FOR
IDENTIFYING NATURAL LANGUAGE
PRESUPPOSITIONS IN ENGLISH

Our purpose in presenting the material in this appendix is to indicate the scope and complexity of the natural language phenomenon of presuppositions. In addition, by listing some of the more common syntactic environments in which presuppositions occur, we provide an opportunity to practice for those students who are interested in sharpening their intuitions in recognizing presuppositions. The list of syntactic environments is not exhaustive, and we will not attempt to present any of the theories which have been proposed by different linguists, logicians, semanticists, or philosophers to account for presuppositions. Rather, our objective is more practical.

At the present time, presuppositions are a major focus of study for a number of linguists, especially linguists who consider themselves Generative Semanticists. In compiling this list of syntactic environments, we have borrowed heavily from the work of Lauri Kartunnen. See the Bibliography for sources.

1. **Simple Presuppositions.**

These are syntactic environments in which the existence of some entity is required for the sentence to make sense (to be either true or false).

    a. **Proper Names.**

        (*George Smith* left the party early.)
        ⟶ (There exists someone named George Smith.) where ⟶ means presupposes.

    b. **Pronouns:** *her, him, they.*

        (I saw *him* leave.) ⟶ (There exists some male [i.e., him].)

    c. **Definite Descriptions.**

        (I liked *the woman with the silver earrings.)*
        ⟶ (There exists a woman with silver earrings.)

    d. **Generic Noun Phrases.**

        Noun arguments standing for a whole class.
        (If *wombats* have no trees in which to climb, they are sad.) ⟶ (There are wombats.)

    e. **Some Quantifiers:** *all, each, every, some, many, few, none.*

        (If *some of the dragons* show up, I'm leaving.) ⟶ (There are dragons.)

2. **Complex Presuppositions.**

Cases in which more than the simple existence of an element is presupposed.

    a. **Relative Clauses.**

        Complex noun arguments, with a noun followed by a phrase beginning with *who,* which, or *that*. (*Several of the women who had spoken to you* left the shop.) ——→ (Several women had spoken to you.)

b. **Subordinate Clauses of Time.**

Classes identified by the cue words *before, after, during, as, since, prior, when, while.* (If the judge was home *when I stopped by her house*, she didn't answer her door.) ——→ (I stopped by the judge's house.)

c. **Cleft Sentence.**

Sentences beginning with It $\left\{ \begin{matrix} was \\ is \end{matrix} \right\}$ noun argument. (It was the extra pressure which shattered the window.)——→(Something shattered the window.)

d. **Pseudo-Cleft Sentences.**

(Identified by the form *What* [Sentence] *is* [sentence]. (What Sharon hopes to do is to become well liked.)——→(Sharon hopes to do something.)

e. **Stressed Sentences.**

Voice stress (If Margaret has talked to THE POLICE, we're finished.)——→(Margaret has talked to someone.)

f. **Complex Adjectives:** *new, old, former, present, previous.*

(If Fredo wears his new ring, I'll be blown away.)——→(Fredo had/has an old ring.)

g. **Ordinal Numerals:** *first, second, third, fourth, another.*

(If you can find a third clue in this letter, I'll make you a mosquito pie.)——→(There are two clues already found.)

h. **Comparatives:** *-er, more, less.*

    (If you know bet*ter* riders than Sue does, tell me who they are.)──→(Sue knows [at least] one rider.) (If you know bet*ter* riders than Sue is, tell me who they are.) ──→ (Sue is a rider.)

i. **Comparative As:** *As x as . . . .*

    (If her daughter is *as funny as* her husband is, we'll all enjoy ourselves.)──→(Her husband is funny.)

j. **Repetitive Cue Words:** *too, also, either, again, back.*

    (If she tells me that *again,* I'll kiss her.) ──→(She has told me that before.)

k. **Repetitive Verbs and Adverbs.**

    Verbs and adverbs beginning with *re-,* e.g., *repeatedly, return, restore, retell, replace, renew.* (If he *returns* before I leave, I want to talk to him.)──→(He has been here before.)

l. **Qualifiers:** *only, even, except, just.*

    (*Only* Amy saw the bank robbers.)──→ (Amy saw the bank robbers.)

m. **Change-of-Place Verbs:** *come, go, leave, arrive, depart, enter.*

    (If Sam has *left* home, he is lost.)──→ (Sam has been at home.)

n. **Change-of-Time Verbs and Adverbs:** *begin, end, stop, start, continue, proceed, already, yet, still, anymore.*

    (My bet is that Harry will *continue* to smile.)──→(Harry has been smiling.)

o. Change-of-State Verbs: *change, transform, turn into, become.*

> (If Mae *turns into* a hippie, I'll be surprised.)
> ———▶ (Mae is not now a hippie.)

p. Factive Verbs and Adjectives: *odd, aware, know, realize, regret.*

> (It is *odd* that she called Maxine at midnight.)———▶(She called Maxine at midnight.)

q. Commentary Adjectives and Adverbs: *lucky, fortunately, far out, out of sight, groovy, bitchin'. . . innocently, happily, necessarily.*

> (It's *far out* that you understand your dog's feelings.)———▶(You understand your dog's feelings.)

r. Counterfactual Conditional Clauses.

> Verbs having subjunctive tense. (*If you had listened to me and your father,* you wouldn't be in the wonderful position you're in now.)———▶ (You didn't listen to me and your father.)

s. Contrary-to-Expectation: *should.*

> (*If you should [happen to]* decide you want to talk to me, I'll be hanging out in the city dump.)———▶ (I don't expect you to want to talk to me.)

t. Selectional Restrictions.

> (If my professor gets *pregnant,* I'll be disappointed.)———▶(My professor is a woman.)

u. Questions.

> (Who ate the tapes?)———▶(Someone ate

the tapes.) (I want to know who ate the tapes.)———▶ (Someone ate the tapes.)

v. **Negative Questions.**

(Did*n't* you want to talk to me?)———▶ (I thought that you wanted to talk to me.)

w. **Rhetorical Questions.**

(Who cares whether you show up or not?) ———▶ (Nobody cares whether you show up or not.)

x. **Spurious:** *not.*

(I wonder if you're not being a little unfair.)———▶ (I think that you're being unfair.)